TEA

640

INY
EX

18

4

AHARI

GKG
3.5
T
2.5

N

1.

CHAI

CHAI

The Experience of Indian Tea

Rekha Sarin · **Rajan Kapoor**

NIYOGI
BOOKS

Overseas Distribution

USA and Canada
ACC Distribution
email: sales@accdistribution.com
www.accdistribution.com

United Kingdom, Ireland, Europe and Africa
Kodansha Europe Ltd
email: info@kodansha.eu
www.kodansha.eu

Cambodia, Burma, Laos and Thailand
Paragon Asia Co. Ltd
email: info@paragonasia.com
www.paragonasia.com

Published by

NIYOGI BOOKS

D-78, Okhla Industrial Area, Phase-I
New Delhi-110 020, INDIA
Tel: 91-11-26816301, 49327000
Fax: 91-11-26810483, 26813830
email: niyogibooks@gmail.com
website: www.niyogibooksindia.com

Text © Rekha Sarin
Photographs © Rajan Kapoor

Editor: Gita Rajan
Design: Diya Dasgupta
Cover Design: Dinesh Chauhan

ISBN: 978-93-81523-91-9
Publication: 2014

Printed at: Niyogi Offset Pvt. Ltd, New Delhi, India

To the tea leaf pluckers and labourers of the tea gardens in India, for keeping alive the heritage of Indian tea.

…their innocent smiles touched me deeply.

- Rajan Kapoor

In memory of my parents, who taught me to seek the inherent beauty in Life.

And for Lennard Rahul and Dominik Vir, bright sparks of the future .

- Rekha Sarin

Contents

Preface   9

Chai the Indian Way   13
Ever Popular Chai   15
How Tea Came to India   35
Contemporary World of Indian Tea   51

Into the Heartlands of Tea   59
Picturesque Tea Tourism   61
Bounty of Assam   71
Divine Boon of Darjeeling   85
Bonanza of South India   105
Bouquet of Regional Teas   131

From the Leaf to the Sip   151
Plucking the Leaf   153
The Planter's Life   173
From Nature to Man   187
The Tea Taster's Verdict   205

Tea the Universal Brew   221
The Saga of Tea   223
Choices for the Tea Lover   249
A Cupful of Health   263
Recipes with Tea   271
Finally the Perfect Cup of Tea   284

Author Note:
Rajan's Vision / Rekha's Musing   286
Acknowledgements   288
Photo Credits   290
Select Bibliography   291
Glossary   293
Index   297

ABOVE: Flowering trees provide bursts of colour to the sumptuous tea countryside of the Nilgiris in sub-tropical South India.

PREVIOUS PAGE: Umbrellas protect pluckers in a tea garden in Darjeeling where brilliant sunshine and fanciful rain give rise to the world's most remarkable teas.

Preface

During the course of our journey through the world of Tea, we have become ardent admirers of the beverage. No doubt, all tea lovers are passionate about their cup of tea—our perceptions have expanded far beyond. We now behold our cup in a spirit of reverence. Tea is a legacy of mankind, a boon that has resulted in a remarkable synergy between the working of Nature and the intelligence and skill of the human mind and hand.

In this book, therefore, while presenting an insight into the exhilarating aromas and characters of the innumerable varieties of Indian teas, we also seek to highlight the extraordinarily multifarious facets of the brew that impact our daily lives in more ways than one.

Our opening section introduces Chai, as construed and experienced in India, traces the history of its advent to India and highlights the contemporary scenario of the tea industry of India.

In this, our land of social contrasts, tea-drinking culture is a skein that runs through the warp and weft of the multi-ethnic tapestry of Indian society. Moreover, tea is an epitome of Indian hospitality. Be it the handyman who comes to do a repair job at home or the most revered guest, it is offered to all. From roadside tea stalls to luxury hotel lounges, or snazzy tea bars, it is available to all. Chai, thus, makes a national statement.

By the early nineteenth century, during the era of colonialism, the British East India Company was bartering tea with China in exchange for opium being grown in India. This eventually resulted in the Opium Wars as the Chinese, realising their monopoly, began to demand a heavy price for tea in the form of silver bullion. Besotted as they were with tea, the colonists then had no choice but to explore an alternate solution. They undertook all sorts of tribulations to finally discover and realise that the jungles of the Assam Valley in north-east India were home to a very special indigenous variety of tea plant. The watershed moment for tea in this country came on February 12, 1839, when the first ever commercial tea company in the world, the Assam Company, came into being.

India thus, is one of the star players in the annals of tea history, and today it is the largest producer of black tea in the world. It also ranks as the fourth largest exporter in the world, even while accounting domestically for approximately twenty per cent of global consumption.

There is a prolific tea industry that exists in the country, with a magnitude that ranges from business houses who have a large stake with massive hectares of tea plantations that produce millions of kilograms of tea, to small growers who rely on 'bought leaf factories' for their produce; from multinational conglomerates and international brands to local players whose labels find popularity in small towns. The Indian marketplace is accommodating and receptive.

The heartlands of tea are spread over a beautiful and diverse geography that is intrinsic to this vast subcontinent. In our second section of the book, we present these regions that yield a plethora of teas that result from the physical attributes of their varying habitats, each variety being incomparable in character. Where else can you find the robust, rich and malty Assam teas with their zesty strength? Or the delightfully delicate and aromatic Darjeeling teas, produced in this picturesque east Himalayan district that is as exclusive to India as the Champagne district is to France? Or the bright, full bodied teas from the Nilgiris and the Western Ghats that come from the southern parts of the country? Then again, regions like Dooars, Terai and Kangra Valley make their own significant contribution.

Visit a tea plantation and you are in the lap of natural beauty. Besides being refreshed by the finest teas from the gardens, enjoy the pristine environment with spectacular views, gurgling rivers, trekking trails and jungle wildlife. Together with the Indian cultural rainbow of regionally diverse dialects and customs, quaint village homes and local celebrations, the tea trail across India presents

a panorama that is as diverse as the cornucopia of tea characters that emerge from each of these regions.

In the third section we take a look at the transformational journey of the leaf to the sip. Its pages describe the 'flushes' or cycles of growth of the tender green shoots and their final transformation to the familiar black dried tea leaves that we use for our brew. Plucking the young leaves and the buds that go together in the making of the finished tea is an operation that is a selective toil done by the hand, so delicate that it is best performed by the female hand. It cannot be replaced by any form of new-age mechanisation. As such, not many of us realise that there is a massive labour force that plucked thousands of young shoots one-by-one, to eventually yield the finished product of tea as we know it.

Most of the large tea plantations carry forward the heritage of the past. The tea planter is not only responsible to produce a quality cup, but he is also accountable for the welfare of thousands of workers on the plantation, several of them having lived there over generations. Being remote and isolated, these vast plantations are more like self-contained townships.

The actual production of tea leaves involves intelligent evaluation, using temperature-controlled techniques that are employed during withering, rolling, fermentation and drying. The tea is either marketed directly or packed in 'lots' that are put up for tea auctions. Critical to the quality control process is the professional tea taster, who with his expertise, appraises and discriminates a good tea from an average one. He also creates the blends that make up the spectrum of commercial brands.

The final section of the book highlights the universal popularity of the beverage—beginning with tracing the history of tea from its origins in China and its emergence in Europe, it goes on to sum up the appealing aspects of this universally favoured drink. This is a drink that has traversed the passages of time, giving rise to several significant historic events, besides enriching lands with a special culture that is an outcome of individual styles of service and manner of taking to the beverage.

Commencing with its discovery in China by the erudite Chinese emperor, Shen Nung in the year 2737 BC, tea moved on to neighbouring Japan, and spread to Europe through cross-continental maritime activity, finally arriving in England by the middle of the seventeenth century. Soon enough, the drink became a rage. This section presents the several profiles of the beverage that offer the tea lover choices for every mood or occasion.

In fact, simply savour your cup of tea, just the way you like it. Feel good, as studies show that this beverage has substantial health benefits.

If you are adventurous in your tastes, this versatile drink makes a wonderful fusion with other flavours. And what's more, as featured in our chapter on recipes, the delicate flavours of tea can be used to advantage in cooking too.

Tea then is a beverage that deserves appreciation in every measure. As a tribute to this blessing of Nature, we met with several tea professionals and visited many a tea plantation across almost all the tea regions in India to present the manifold aspects of this subject and capture its charming beauty through the lens. In the process, the complexities of this fascinating drink have been a revelation to us, and we now appreciate our daily cup with renewed delight. We hope you, our readers, enjoy participating in the tea experience, page by page, sip by sip.

FACING PAGE: Tea can be taken 'black', or with lemon, or with meagre to generous addition of milk.

CHAI THE **INDIAN** WAY

'I remember my childhood spending wonderful summer months in Shimla,' recollects silver-haired Usha, an octogenarian whose memories burn bright with nostalgia. Her father was an employee under the British government, in the days when the summer capital shifted every year from Delhi to Shimla. 'A part of our daily excitement were the afternoons when we would come rushing out of our homes to the clanging of a bell, sounded by a man on a cycle who called out for everyone to see his demonstration on the preparation of Brooke Bond tea, which he made on a small portable burner.'

FACING PAGE: Chai: drink it your style—be it from a bowl, a mug, a glass or cup—it only gets better with every sip!

EVER POPULAR CHAI

'Come, oh come, ye tea-thirsty restless ones—the kettle boils, bubbles and sings, musically.'

~ Rabindranath Tagore

In India, tea is a way of life. It permeates every strata of society and transcends all barriers of economic disparity—from the gleaming kitchens of the super-rich and upper middle class, whose 'khansama' or cook may bring out an impeccably set tea array, to the humble kitchen of the lower middle class where tea may be had in an unpretentious mug or glass; from the sparse hutment of the labourer, where it remains intrinsic to the shoestring food budget, to the slick corporate boardroom where business honchos make management decisions over a cuppa. Tea holds good everywhere.

This tea drinking habit is a legacy that is left behind by the British colonisers who were the architects of the tea industry in India. Eventually so successful were they and their enterprise took such firm ground, that they did all they could to 'groom' the populace to adopt tea as a household beverage.

Active campaigning to popularise tea was directed towards the locals so that the British could increase their tea business and expand the market. This bequest made by them is now embedded in the Indian mould. The custom of adding milk to tea that was introduced by English high society defines most of the tea consumption patterns throughout the country.

Moreover, there is one common thought that runs like a main skein through the entire fabric of Indian society: tea is an icon of Indian hospitality. What better way of traditional *athithi satkar* or 'honour a guest' than to proffer a cup of tea? Not only that, it is not uncommon

for the plumber or carpenter who visits the average household to do repair jobs to be offered a cup of sweet milky 'chai' by the relieved and kindly mistress of the house. And in all likelihood, such an offer would be accepted with alacrity.

In a nation where society dictates a strong family system, the beverage becomes an excellent catalyst for social bonding and expressive vocal interaction. Nothing like a good chat or gossip over a cup of tea!

It is estimated that the annual per capita consumption of tea in India is around 718 grams; that adds up to approximately 890 million kilograms per year. Almost eighty per cent of the country's total production of 1111.76 million kilograms is consumed at home. This means that if every Indian were to have one more cup of tea per day, there would be hardly any tea left for export. However, the average per head consumption in this country is lower than that in many other countries like the UK, Ireland and the Middle East. Still, India's domestic consumption of tea accounts for approximately twenty per cent of the global consumption of an estimated 4440 million kilograms of tea.

FACING PAGE: Villagers in Rajasthan sip tea as they take a break from the beating sun.

FACING PAGE: This artistically styled ethnic tray at Chor Bizarre restaurant in London, showcases some Indian savouries and cuisine that typically go with the vigorous strength of Indian chai. Chor Bizarre serves a high-tea menu every afternoon when it becomes 'Chai Bizarre', with desserts that are paired with different varieties of tea. In multi-ethnic India, the preparation of tea differs in every region, and it is enjoyed with some typical accompaniments.

OVERLEAF: Delights in a Kashmiri home. Nothing more relaxing than a *hookah* and a sip of *kahwa* with the family. In the centre stands an engraved copper samovar to keep the brew warm.

Tea Culture in Regional kitchen

Be it the snowy winter of the Himalayan states, or the inertia of the summer heat of the flat northern plains, or the indolence of the sultry monsoon humidity of the eastern region and the coastal ghats—every climatic belt provides a good reason for indulging in the reviving properties of the brew.

As this is a vast country with heterogeneous lifestyles, each regional kitchen has its own interpretation on the preparation and serving of tea. Take for instance, Ladakh, the 'Roof of India', where the dizzying heights of this high altitude cold desert are dictated by a culture very similar to that of Central Asia.

Here, local kitchens prepare tea by churning together green tea (a variety of tea preferred in the hilly regions rather than the universally popular black tea), yak butter, and salt. The preparation emits a rumbling sound while it is being mixed, and this results in its given name, *gurgur cha*.

In the beautiful Himalayan vale of Kashmir, tea takes on a unique aspect. Better known as *kahwa*, it is prepared from green tea leaf. Each ingredient used in the *kahwa* reflects their daily way of life. Crushed cardamom and cinnamon are first added to the boiling water, infusing it with a strong aroma that combats the slightly grassy quality of green tea. These ingredients also promote digestion, and as Kashmiri food is rich, a formal *wazwan* or banquet is never considered complete without *kahwa*. Saffron is also added to the tea, as this grows abundantly in the Valley. So too, the topping of slivered almonds; they come from the almond trees that thrive here. Traditionally the tea is brewed in a samovar, with a separate place in the centre for burning charcoal, so that the brew is kept boiling all the time. Locals sometimes drink another type of tea called *noon* chai. In this case, salt is added instead of sugar together with a pinch of sodium bi-carbonate. The tea looks pink in colour, and is topped with a thick layer of cream.

Elsewhere in India, green tea is relatively limited in demand, and it is only of late that it has come into favour amongst urban tea drinkers. Most north Indian homes prefer the more common black tea to which milk is added, and many kitchens concoct 'readymade' tea, a mix of tea leaves, milk and sugar, all boiled together in a pan. They also make a popular variation, *masala* chai, in which spices like crushed cardamom, cloves and cinnamon are added to the boiling concoction, at times also adding ginger and black pepper. In Punjab, a land whose hearty people have a preference for heavy foods, a traditional breakfast starts with fried stuffed paranthas, washed down with 'readymade' chai. Just as cakes and sandwiches are traditional accompaniments to English tea, there are Indian accompaniments that go with tea as well. Some familiar savouries include *pakoda*s and samosas, while commonly-served sweets like *jalebi*s, *rasgulla*s and *gulab jamun*s are always popular on the tea menu in any local restaurant, big or small.

Closer to the tea gardens in West Bengal, the preparation of tea in a Kolkata home takes on more of the English culture, as the city was the first bastion of colonisation. Bengalis like to emphasise on flavour, allowing the tea to brew to the correct degree in the teapot, and would never go for a mixed concoction of tea and milk. In South India, where coffee tends to be popular, people like strong flavours. As a result, they use 'tea dust', (the smallest particles of tea leaves that result during manufacture) that is tied in a muslin cloth and swirled in boiling water, to give a dark brew, taken with milk.

LEFT: A local prepares the salty *gurgur cha* in Rombak, Ladakh.

ABOVE: A Kashmiri warms up with *noon* chai or salty tea.
BELOW Locals in Pahalgam, Kashmir, await their serving of the brew being prepared and dispensed from a samovar.

ABOVE: Buddhist monks in the hills of Dharamshala, Kangra, refresh themselves with tea before resuming their monastic routine.

BELOW: Tea provides a sojourn for a lively discussion at Dolly's Tea Shop in Kolkata.

FACING PAGE: Roadside tea in Kolkata is served in *kullads*, the unglazed terracotta cups that can be thrown away after use. Clay handicrafts are a part of local culture.

Chai and Dhaba Culture

Go along the humming streets of any metropolis or pause at any of the small towns and villages along the highway and you are sure to find the omnipresent tea stall or dhaba. It will be usually abuzz with a knot of people sipping their tea most likely with slurping sounds of relish—the common man's expression of respite from the drudgery of routine.

At the break of dawn, mid-noon, post-lunch or in the evening, and in some cases, even late into the night, the kettle remains on the boil, in constant complicity with its many takers. It seems that the man-on-the-street likes his tea prepared quite differently from the customary methods of preparation in an urban home. This is 'chai' in its true ethnic sense. However, here too, with each region the manner of tea drinking varies.

In North India, a tea stall may sometimes be just a wooden trolley, set up under the shade of a leafy tree. It is a sort of mobile kitchen, equipped with a gas cylinder which is kept below the trolley in order to feed the stove on top. Tea is made in a long-handled pan that has invariably been blackened with use. Water, milk, sugar and the tea leaves are all added together at the same time. As the concoction comes to a boil and froths, it is deftly lifted and swirled and put right back on the flame, only to boil again and again. The 'cooked' tea is then poured with aplomb through a large strainer into the glass and the tea-leaf residue is promptly dunked back into the pan.

A second stove might already have a mixture of water and milk on the boil, and this is added to the first pan, so that the tea leaves get re-used. Milk has its own entity and it submerges the increasingly strong taste of the cooked and re-cooked tea.

Eventually, the constantly bubbling preparation adopts a thick, syrupy consistency, with the sharp sweetness of sugar. It becomes heavy and filling, so that for a poor man, it becomes a sort of an affordable 'meal in a cup'. However, dhabas usually sell tea in a thick 'half glass' and not in a cup.

Nowadays plastic half glasses are being increasingly used, heralding the modernisation of the tea stall. Still, it is here that the common man enjoys taking his break, any place and any time.

ABOVE: The chai-wallah pours tea from one pan to another in long movements to give the brew a frothy head.

FACING PAGE: A member of the Sikh community doles out early morning tea to labourers, in Chandni Chowk, Old Delhi.

It is 7:00 a.m. on a cold February morning and around Jama Masjid in the old city of Delhi, the tea stalls, of which there are several, are going about their sprightly morning business. In places some of the vendors have simply placed small stoves on the pavements against the backdrop of shuttered shops but even these seem to be thriving. No one is in competition. Labourers, rickshaw-wallahs, handcart pullers, and burqua-clad mothers in purdah walking their children to school, are all ready to fortify themselves with chai. Some dhabas have boiled eggs and buns as breakfast accompaniments. Most display jars of long rusks that are popularly dipped into the beverage. As the day progresses, the place will be choked with the rush of traders and shoppers, this being the traditional hub of wholesale commercial activity. There will be many more takers for tea.

Ahmad Aziz's tea-shop does brisk business. He has two price ranges: a 'single chai' at a nominal price, while a 'double chai' fetches twice the price. The latter is cooked entirely in milk. Both the varieties are so much in demand that he even employs a runner who delivers glasses of tea that sit tightly packed in a special wire container, to the surrounding guesthouses and the local shops.

Aziz's daily procurement bill includes a massive average of eighty kilograms of milk, twelve to thirteen kilograms of sugar, and two to three kilograms of tea leaves. Not only is this due to the customer footfall, but it also proclaims the process of making the chai: liberal quantities of milk and sugar, as compared to a relatively small proportion of tea leaves that are used over and over again in the constantly boiling brew.

Further on, as the sun rises over Chandni Chowk, on the boulevard leading off the famous Red Fort, a line of labourers wait for tea being doled out from a gigantic kettle aboard a moving van that is manned by Sikhs from their sanctified place of worship nearby, the Sisganj Gurudwara. This is an act of *sewa* or social service, as propounded in their scriptures; tea is their link to humanity.

Then again, moving to the new and posh area of South Delhi, take the example of Dashrath, who runs his tea stall in a lane behind a Handicrafts Emporium that is frequented by tourists. He has been given the contract to supply glasses of tea that the emporium offers to its customers. This customary Indian hospitality that even permeates business, secures a steady income for Dashrath, in addition to the several walk-in customers from the street. He adapts his tea to suit the clients, sometimes making cardamom tea or even tea without milk, on demand.

Roadside chai also takes on the form of sixty-mile chai or 'trucker's tea' served in dhabas along the immense highway network that links the populous cities in the North. Sturdy truck drivers ply their vehicles through the night stopping by at these dhabas that are located usually next to petrol pumps. Gaily festooned with bright lights strung out like beacons in the dark, they offer a meal of lentils and curries the flavours of which are honed by being cooked over a slow charcoal fire and are accompanied by hot tandoori roti made in a clay oven. This fare is topped with tea so strong that it guarantees to keep sleep at bay for at least the next sixty miles.

ABOVE: Hindu sadhus at the momentous Ardh Kumbh Mela in Haridwar, paused to take dhaba chai and pose for the camera. A young sadhu from the Juna *akhara* (brotherhood) wears an inscrutable smile as he holds his glass of tea.

Regional India and Roadside Tea

In India, more especially so in North India, the culture of roadside tea drinking is an activity people from all walks of life enjoy, irrespective of caste, class or status. It is akin to the participation in fairs like the Kumbh Mela, the Ardh Kumbh Mela and the like where both the householder and the sadhu who has renounced all, join in with equal gusto, full of faith and fervour.

The Kumbh Mela celebrates a Vedic myth that Lord Vishnu, the Creator, spearheaded the gods to defeat the demons and snatched away the *kumbh*, the pot that contained *amrit*, the Nectar of Immortality. Drops of *amrit* fell over the waters at four places, Allahabad, Ujjain, Nashik and Haridwar. Millions of pilgrims, led by sadhus and sages take a dip in these waters with great religious zeal to purify themselves. This mammoth bathing jamboree is held four times, every twelve years, in rotation among the four places. As a scientific explanation, the constellation of the stars during this period is supposed to cast an influence on the waters that acquire healing qualities for certain diseases. Ardh Kumbh or 'half a pot' is held only in Allahabad and Haridwar every sixth year.

Several Hindu sadhus congregate during the Kumbh Mela. Their temples besmirched in red, signify Shakti, the Hindu Goddess who represents the cosmic energy of power. Often their headgears and outfits are made of rudraksha beads, which are supposed to be the eyes of Lord Shiva, or power beads of the Vedic gods. Some sadhus claim to heal people with their tantric powers and the sacred bones they carry with them.

Moving east, towards Kolkata, the tea capital of India, dhaba culture takes on the aspect of serving the beverage in earthen *kullads*. The city itself lies on the banks of the river Hooghly which meets the silt-laden Ganges, whose huge deposits of reddish clay are used to create some beautiful terracotta handicrafts and hence the *kullads*, small rounded unglazed cups without handles that can be thrown away after use. One finds tea trolleys stationed on the pulsating pavements every few yards in the commercial areas. A few sips of the strong dhaba

ABOVE: A sadhu enjoys his chai at the Kumbh Mela.
BELOW: Ramdas Baba wears a necklace of human bones that have been retrieved from cremation grounds.

chai, sometimes served in a miniscule *kullad*, is enough to revive sagging energy in the face of the ever-present humidity. Besides, the average Bengali man-on-the-street is always ready to break for tea with a leisurely discussion on politics.

Russel Punjabi Dhaba in Kolkata is a hot spot where even the well-heeled stop by to enjoy tea with savoury samosas. This is where Indian tea culture reflects the remnants of the past, as some of the city streets still carry British names, and so does this long-standing tea stall that is run by a Sikh migrant.

This British-ethnic appellation is curious to West Bengal. The old English street names remain the same, but the home-grown dhaba is classically local, complete with samosas served with the tea.

While on this culture of contrasts, it is irresistible to digress and mention Firpo's on nearby Park Street, a tea-room that belongs to the days of the Raj, and still has the old-world ambience of mirrored walls and glittering lights. It serves tea the English way, in the pot, with some excellent tea-time snacks.

The local interpretation of tea in neighbouring Assam is quite different. Here, typical chai is strong and salty instead of sweet.

It is infused with the flavour of *adrak* and *tejpatta* (ginger and bay leaf), and locals maintain that tea prepared in this manner wards off malaria, a disease that is rampant in this tropical region.

The norm is to sip the chai in a large metal bowl called *banbati* rather than in a cup or glass.

In the South, although tea stalls exist aplenty, they are quieter, and do not offer the elaborate fare that is found in North Indian dhabas. They only serve breakfast, with potato *bondas*, local pastry puffs or a hard bread called *porai*, best eaten softened by dipping into the tea.

A good prototype is Moosa Tea Stall in Chennai. Located in the old Fort St. George area behind the railway station on bustling Walltax road off Broadway, this shop has been in the business of making tea for more than thirty years, and has never lost its popularity. It draws two to three hundred customers every day.

The tea stall vendor places a few hundred grams of Brooke Bond Super Dust tea at the bottom of a cloth bag tied to a long-handled strainer. This is dipped and swirled into the boiling solution of an equal proportion of milk and water. He adds a liberal amount of sugar into a large mug, and then pours the tea through the strainer into the glass, which he swiftly tips into the mug. The tea is dexterously poured from mug to glass and vice versa in rapid movements, so the liquid appears almost to hang in mid-air. Finally he sets down the tea, with a layer of frothy bubbles, below which the brew retains its ideal temperature.

FACING PAGE: Russel Punjabi Dhaba in Kolkata is a hot spot.

ABOVE: A dhaba runner in Delhi fits glasses of tea into a wire container for delivery.

BELOW: This dhaba tea stall does brisk business on a cold winter morning in Delhi.

In Kerala, *masala* chai is served with the added zest of crushed black peppercorns and in some cases, nutmeg is also added to the green cardamom and cinnamon that go into the tea. This is the homeland of spices, and the ethnic style of tea preparation is defined by these additions that are a produce of this lush tropical state.

However in general, as coffee is the predominant beverage, dhabas in South India are not as common as in the North. Instead, 'tiffin rooms' are more frequented.

They are a throwback on the days of the Raj, evolving from the term 'tiffing' that is, drinking, usually tea, at breakfast or lunch. As such, tiffin rooms are more in the nature of canteens, by way of atmosphere and pricing. They open early for breakfast with tea and coffee served with *idlis*, *vadas* and *upma*.

In the Deccan city of Hyderabad, the chai dhaba is supplanted by Irani restaurants. These have been set up by Zoroastrian immigrants from Iran who fled religious persecution during the nineteenth century and were given protection by the Nizam. As they lacked the capital to do trading or commerce, they resorted to setting up modest cafés. These had their own unique distinctive ambience with high ceilings and marble-topped tables.

'Sadly nowadays, these are nearing extinction in the face of the realty explosion where developers lure the restaurant owners into giving up their property for attractive monetary offers,' laments M. Gautham Swamy a 'Hyderabadi' resident. He reminisces, 'Having tea in an Irani restaurant especially after a game of morning tennis was a special experience. You asked for *khade chamach ki chai* meaning that the tea had so much sugar in it that a spoon could stand in the cup!' The tea was accompanied by special salty-sweet Osmania biscuits.

The Iranis first came to Mumbai, where they found affinity with the Parsi Zoroastrians. Cafés run by them are also sadly diminishing as a part of a fading culture. They make a strong tea, boiled with milk together with sweetened condensed milk. Service is brisk, with waiters calling out orders of food favourites like bun *maska* with scrambled egg *akuri*, vegetable puff or spicy *dhansak*.

In the neighbouring state of Gujarat, there is another variation of dhaba tea. Once again, leaf dust is used here, and it is kept on the boil, mixed with milk and

ABOVE: The roadside signboard translates the dynamism of India, where the popularity of tea vies with Cola culture.
FACING PAGE: A tea stall outside a bustling bus stop in Coonoor offers chai with popular snacks like chick-pea batter fried chilli *pakoda*s and *vadai*.

stirred continuously with a brass ladle until the quantity is reduced to less than half. By then, the metallic ladle has also imparted a different kind of flavour to the tea. It is then sloshed into a small cup with a saucer, notwithstanding the fact that most of it overruns into the saucer. That, perhaps, is the sheer delight of enjoying tea on the roadside.

There is also the concept of *adha*, or half-a-cup. And to try that 'special' chai, which is even more generously laced with milk, speak in the colloquial language of the tea stall vendor, and ask him to make it *pecial*, a corruption of the word 'special' absorbed into the local lingo.

The extraordinarily milky content of Gujarati tea may be attributed to the prevalence of large-scale dairy farming in this state.

In next-door Rajasthan, dhabas prepare tea that is bright and strong. The brew is served with a liberal amount of sugar that perhaps helps to combat fatigue from the intense heat in this desert state. Each region thus brings its own nuances to the preparation of the beverage.

The early Chinese dialect used words such as *Tchai*, *Cha* and *Tay* to describe both the beverage and the leaf, and these were forerunners of the word 'tea' used for the beverage in its varied forms across most languages of the world. The Chinese words were assimilated in their near original form in many Indian languages especially those of the major tea drinking states of India.

There is the colloquial expression, *chai-paani*, that infers to a 'tip'. And if a worker, having done his job, uses this term, he is hinting for that little 'extra' remuneration. Chai, in India, can mean much more!

FACING PAGE : Tea and intimate talks go hand-in-hand.
ABOVE: A tea table embodying style and social grace at a
home in New Delhi, India.

HOW TEA CAME TO INDIA

*'Steam rises from a cup of tea and we are wrapped in history,
inhaling ancient times and lands, comfort of ages in our hands.'*

~ *Faith Greenbowl*

May 8, 1838

With bated breath, tea lovers in London awaited the arrival of the sailing ship, *Calcutta*, to offload its first ever cargo of tea that had been manufactured in India, a faraway land where the enterprising East India Company, under the patronage of the Crown, was holding increasing political sway. The cargo was precious, as this small consignment was in effect, the chronicle of a bold struggle by British pioneers to grow tea in the sub-tropical north-eastern regions of Assam.

Way back in 1788, Sir Joseph Banks, an acknowledged botanist and president of the Royal Society in England, had first suggested that the climate in Assam could lend itself to tea cultivation. The Company's Board of Directors, however, showed little interest as they preferred to give precedence to their sources of supply from China which hinged on the convenient 'exchange and barter' with illicit opium grown in India. It was only after the Opium Wars that the Crown began to recognise the necessity of encouraging the production of tea elsewhere in the Empire.

The monopoly of China over tea production had to be broken. And what better way to do that than explore the possibility of cultivation in a neighbouring nation, viz. India, that was under the control of the British Empire through the East India Company! Thus began the search, first with scepticism and then with optimism, to finally result in success.

The Search in Upper Assam

Meanwhile, the tea plant had always existed in India. It simply grew unacknowledged in the jungles of Assam. It is hard to imagine that the now familiar image of the neatly-pruned tea bush was, in its original form, a vigorous wild tree that grew to a height of 600–700 cm, and bears leaves as large as 20–22 cm in length and 10 cm in breadth.

It was in these jungles that the earliest tea drinkers, the Singhpo and Khamti tribes lived, and it was Bisa Gaum, the Singhpo chief whom Robert Bruce, a Scottish tradesman first met in 1823 to explore the potential of tea. He had got the lead from Maniram Dutta Barua, a native nobleman close to the Raja of Assam. Bruce was excited, knowing full well that if tea could be produced elsewhere than China, it would make history.

However, it would take several years of trial and experimentation for the British colonisers to recognise these seeds as tea as the Assam variety differs in character, being larger and more robust than the China variety that was familiar so far.

Unfortunately, Robert Bruce died the following year and it was left to his brother, Captain Charles Alexander

FACING PAGE: A tea poster of colonial times apparently meant to draw the French market to teas from the far off land of Darjeeling.

Bruce, an officer with the British gunboats in the Burma War, to deliver the specimens to the 'agent' in Assam. However, the superintendent of the Calcutta Botanical Garden, Dr Nathanial Wallich, to whom these specimens were sent, refused to acknowledge these as real tea.

When, in 1833, a special Tea Committee was set up under the Governor-General Lord William Bentinck, the matter was taken up again and this time, under the directive of the new agent, Francis Jenkins, Lieutenant Andrew Charlton was sent to Upper Assam to collect the indigenous plants. He declared his findings as positive and now Dr Wallich was ready to re-consider his views. He recommended deputing of 'scientific gentlemen' to investigate 'botanical, geological and other details of Upper Assam.' (Androbus: 1957).

Thus began a serious expedition comprising Dr N. Wallich, J. McClelland, a geologist and W. Griffiths, a botanist. The expedition left Calcutta on August 29, 1835. They arrived at Sadiya in Tinsukia in Assam in January next year. From here they made their journey into the depths of Singpho territory on elephants, in boats, or simply by foot, making extensive observations. Griffiths recorded their findings in his journals and noted McClelland's observations.

> '...if we take Kiang-nan and Kiang-see as instance of two of the Tea provinces (in China) of which we have the best information, we find their resemblance in all great leading features to Assam, very remarkable.' (Griffiths: n. p.)

The last stop of the expedition was at Rungagurrah, where they met the native chief *Burra-Senaputtee* or 'Big Warrior' in the village of Tingrei and saw how the Singpho made the tea, using only the young leaves. By the time the expedition was over, it was confirmed that the tea plant was indeed indigenous to Assam.

Still, it was felt that the Chinese seed was superior and so G.J. Gordon, Secretary of the Tea Committee, was dispatched to China to collect 'seeds and plants of the very best stocks'. He returned with 80,000 seeds, of which 20,000 seeds were planted in the Botanical Gardens of Calcutta, and the rest sent in equal ratios to Assam, the hills of Darjeeling and down south to the Madras Presidency. None of the plants survived in Calcutta, nor did they take to the heat in Assam or in the southern regions.

Meanwhile, Charles Bruce's indigenous tea plants in the nurseries at Sadiya had survived. Finally, Wallich was convinced about the quality of the Indian tea plant. He wrote:

> '... as a very eligible spot was selected by Mr McClelland behind that of Mr Bruce's, the plants were subsequently removed thither, together with some plants of Mr Bruce's seeds of indigenous stock were likewise sown. From these shrubs the first tea ever made by Chinese in British India was produced and although the supply was small, yet I am not aware of its having proved inferior to any subsequently manufactured.' (Androbus: 1957).

Unfortunately C.A. Bruce was never given credit for his efforts to establish that fine tea could be produced from the indigenous tea plant. Still, he wrote: 'Should what I have written on this new and interesting subject...enrich our own dominions and pull down the haughty pride of China, I shall feel myself richly repaid for all the perils and dangers and fatigues that I have undergone for the cause of British India Tea.' (Report of 1839, Androbus: 1951).

Ironically, praise for sourcing the tea plant was accorded to Lieutenant Charlton and Jenkins and they were awarded gold medals in 1842. Although C.A. Bruce had been unceremoniously ignored, he had carried on making tenacious efforts to make tea with the help of two Chinese tea makers that he recruited. He sent a sample dispatch for approval to the Viceroy, Lord Auckland, and a consignment of forty-six chests was sent to the Tea Committee in London aboard the *Calcutta* in 1837. Of this, a large portion got mouldy in transit and finally only eight chests of tea were off loaded in the docks.

The Court of Directors of the East India Company— besides famous tea connoisseurs like W. J. Thompson, Richard Twining, Richard Gibbs, Sanderson, Frys Fox & Company—inspected and approved the tea.

FACING PAGE: [CLOCKWISE FROM TOP LEFT]
Gravestone of Charles Alexander Bruce at Pertabghur Tea Estate near Tezpur, Assam;
'Rang Ghar' in Sibasagar, a pavilion and amphitheater built by the Ahom kings to watch sport; believed to be the first of its kind in Asia;
The now familiar tea bush originally grew to the height of a sturdy tree.

The Assam Company is Born

The Brahmaputra Valley became known in England and entrepreneurs in London and Calcutta saw a great business opportunity here. A Provisional Committee was set up to pass a resolution calling for the formation of a company that would lease out tracts of land in Assam for tea cultivation. It had an authorised capital of £500,000 in 10,000 shares of £50 each. Of these, 8,000 shares were offered to investors in England, and the remaining 2,000 in India.

Finally, amidst great euphoria, on February 12, 1839, through a Deed of British Parliament, the world's first ever tea company, The Assam Company, came into being. Simultaneously, another company called the Bengal Tea Association was formed in Calcutta. Amongst its nine directors were members of the offices of Carr, Tagore & Company—William Carr, William Princep and Dwarakanath Tagore (grandfather of poet and Nobel Laureate Rabindranath Tagore), an eminent personality of those times.

Soon the two companies merged under the name of The Assam Company. It was unique in being the first joint stock company with shareholders in London as well as Calcutta, although it was the London directors who actually controlled the purse-strings.

In August 1839, the company set up headquarters in Nazira, in the north-eastern district of Assam. C.A. Bruce and J. Parker were appointed 'Superintendents of Tea Culture'.

After some initial setbacks, the company did so well that Queen Victoria even directed her Court to favour tea from Assam rather than China.

Full recognition came when the Assam Company was incorporated by Parliament with Act No: XIX of 1845. Its original seal read: 'Ingenio et Labore', that is, 'Ingenuity and Hard Work'.

The efforts of the discovery had been fittingly acknowledged. By this time it was decided with full confidence, that all plantings in this region should be made with seedlings from the native tea bushes and over the ensuing years, the British-India tea began to flourish.

Setting up the Tea Gardens

Cultivating the very first tea gardens was a challenge for the brave-hearted. The pioneers hacked through thick jungles, burning and clearing tracts of land in the face of constant threat from wild animals like tigers, leopards and wolves. The climate was alien and harsh and the incidence of life-threatening diseases like malaria, cholera and dysentery was high.

Still this did not deter a number of other investors to form companies like the Jorhat Tea Company in 1859, and proprietary gardens were established in other districts like Cachar as well. In 1844, the East India Company had purchased its first two steamers, the *Assam* and the *Naga* from the Assam Company, which plied from Calcutta to Gauhati (now Guwahati). Nevertheless, it took over three months to reach the plantations as the journey had first to be made up the river Brahmaputra by slow country boat, and then the final lap covered on elephants through tiger-infested country.

As the region developed, by 1885, the Dibrugarh-Sadiya rail and the Jorhat Provincial Railway lines had been laid.

In 1890, the journey from Calcutta to Dibrugarh used to take a fortnight, in 1904 it took three days, and by 1940, it took thirty hours by rail.

From a time when river services were the only means of transportation to the present day, when the journey can be done in a matter of hours by air, this extreme north-eastern pioneering region of tea in India has seen it all.

FACING PAGE: [TOP] A share certificate of the Assam Company, the world's first ever commercial tea company formed by a Deed of British Parliament on February 12, 1839.
[BELOW LEFT TO RIGHT] Nathanial Wallich, a botanist of Dutch origin; Lord Auckland, Governor-General of British India 1836–1842, under whom tea forays in Assam got underway; Robert Fortune, a Scottish botanist and enthusiastic plant hunter, who disguised himself as a Chinaman.
OVERLEAF: A tea estate in the flatlands of Assam.

FIRST SHARE CERTIFICATE

ASSAM COMPANY.

BENGAL BRANCH

ESTABLISHED IN **1839** UPON A CAPITAL

The Indian Contribution

Even today, the original tea drinkers of India, the Singphos, take pride that they were generations ahead of the British colonisers in their knowledge of tea. It is said that it was Chief Bisa Gaum's army that really gave the planters the idea of pruning when they slashed the bushes in protest against the British imposing royalty. A tea garden called 'Bessakopie' still exists, and its name translates as 'where Bisa chopped off the tea plants'. In the Tinsukia district of Assam, the Singphos continue to grow tea in their village homes as a tradition, and make a brew of smoked tea leaves apart from using them in their cooking.

Indian initiatives for the development of the local tea enterprise would have been much greater, had they not been doused by the tragic end of Maniram Dutta Barua. A man of brilliance, he joined the newly formed Assam Company as a Dewan or land agent. In 1845, he resigned to set up his own tea plantations, but the colonialists could not tolerate any inititative or competition from the local entrepreneurs.

When, in 1857, the Indian Mutiny broke out all over as an expression of the 'First War of Independence', Maniram Dewan—as he was by then known—was arrested in Calcutta where he had gone to represent Raja Purinder Singha of Assam and petition for his grievances. He was hanged on February 26, 1858, a

move that was actually meant to be an ominous warning to other aspiring 'native' entrepreneurs who wished to enter the tea industry. Dewan is therefore considered the 'Martyr of Indian Tea', having brought to notice the existence of the tea plant in India, for which he paid dearly, with his life.

Tea Moves on to Darjeeling

In 1839, a civil surgeon, Dr Campbell, was transferred from Kathmandu as Superintendent of the newly acquired region of Darjeeling for which the British had manoeuvred a lease from the Maharaja of Sikkim in return for a small subsidy. They had realised the suitability of these salubrious hills for a sanatorium. However, these cool climes would prove to be more of a success for planting tea. For, the doctor felt rather lonely and in a bid to attract settlers, decided to start a new venture and sowed some tea seeds near his residence at Beechwood. Soon these were flourishing and in 1847, the government decided to develop tea nurseries in this area.

Here too, planters made gruelling journeys in search of land for developing tea plantations. When Dr Joseph Hooker, a naturalist friend of Charles Darwin, ventured to establish a tea garden at Lebong in 1848, he was carried in a palanquin 'comprising a long box with a shutter' during his journey from Calcutta to Darjeeling. The palanquin was borne on four poles and carried by bearers who crossed ravines, streams and leech-covered jungles to reach the site for tea plantation (based on the account by Moxham: 2003).

By 1852, so desperate was the East India Company to break the Chinese monopoly over tea, that Robert Fortune, a Scottish botanist and traveller who spoke fluent Chinese, was enlisted to penetrate the secret gardens of China, from where he managed to obtain some 20,000 plants of the best black and green tea for plantations in Darjeeling.

Within a decade, over a hundred tea gardens were flourishing in Darjeeling district. Some, like the Darjeeling Consolidated Tea Company, which was established in 1896, had huge operations.

LEFT: Maniram Dewan, the 'Martyr of Indian Tea'.
FACING PAGE: An unfurling tea bud. British planters observed that the Singphos made tea from only new shoots.

By this time it was realised that tea cultivation could be extended to other surrounding areas such as Terai in the Himalayan foothills. The first such plantation, Champta Planting, was set up in 1862. It was later extended to the Dooars, where the Assamese tea bush proved to be better suited. Gazeldubi was the first garden and by 1876 this area had thirteen plantation.

Tea Ventures in the North-West

After the Darjeeling success, there was growing optimism that tea could be grown in places like Kangra at the foot of the Western Himalayas. The area was a part of the North-West Frontier Province and in 1849, when Dr Jameson, Superintendent of the Botanical Gardens in Peshawar visited this district, he found the lower elevations of the Dhauladhar range in the Kangra Valley here conducive for tea cultivation. The following note reiteretes, '...future prospects of the planters appear very satisfactory...the climate of the valley and of adjacent tracts...is extremely well adapted for tea; (Gazetteer of the Kangra District 1883–84 Vol 1: Aug 2001). He planted the China variety of seeds and the

first commercial plantation was established at Holta near Palampur in 1852. Tea was also grown in small measure in the valleys of Kumaon, Kullu and Garhwal. The pioneering hardships of the early days were now being compensated by the taste of success.

A Buddhist myth attributes tea to Prince Bodhi Dharma in India, who cut off his eyelids to prevent sleep during meditation, and where they fell to the ground, a tea bush sprouted.

Tea Goes to South India

Down south in the Madras Presidency, Gordon's trial consignment of Chinese seedlings was sent to the newly developed town of Ootacamund or 'Ooty' that lay in the Nilgiris, where the Collector, Madras Presidency of British India, had created his retreat, Stone House, in 1823.

The seedlings were first planted on an experimental farm in Ketti Valley in the Nilgris around Ooty, under the supervision of a French botanist, M. Perrottet. By 1839

these were doing exceedingly well and the British settlers soon realised that the entire area between the Western Ghats and the Arabian Sea presented a great potential for tea. To set up the plantations, they made hazardous journeys, similar to those in the North-east, through thick rainforests infested with dangerous wildlife. In 1854, Mann started a plantation near Coonoor, and became the first to manufacture Nilgiri tea.

It would take another five years for really large-scale plantations to come up, and the first of these were Thiashola and Dunsandle Estates near Kulhatty. By 1926, tea had extended to the southern most tip of the hilly ghats with the establishment of large companies like the Bombay Burmah Trading Corporation Limited (BBTCL). Incorporated in 1863, this was the first 'Rupee company' with public participation founded in India and had started by trading in timber from Burma.

The last planting district to be opened up was the High Wavys, hills deep down in the Western Ghats, where in 1927, Napier Ford first planted tea on Cloudland Estate.

FACING PAGE: Kangra Valley in the Dhauladhar Mountain ranges of the Western Himalayas.

ABOVE: A tea estate in South India is distinguished by betel nut palms growing in its valley.

LEFT: Tea pluckers negotiate a steep slope in Darjeeling. China seedlings proved a success here.

RIGHT: A eucalyptus tree grows by a tea slope in the Nilgiris.

The Intrepid Marwaris

Indigenous planters in Assam venturing into tea cultivation were not too many, considering the sad fate of Maniram Dutta Barua. There were only a few bold hearted, like Rosheswar Barua, who managed to establish six tea estates. Still, the enterprising spirit of the Marwari community remained unfazed. With their inherent penchant for trade and finance, they navigated the long distance from their native western states of Marwar and Rajasthan on camel back or even on foot, traversing unyielding lands to try their luck in Calcutta and Assam. As the local Assamese did not show much enterprise, they learned all the ropes and took over trade and business in this region.

'There is gold growing there—why don't you go and see for yourself,' is what Senai Ram Lohia was told, sometime in the year 1865, by a Rajput from his native village who had joined the British army in Assam, recalls Ashok Kumar Lohia, Chairman of the Kolkata-based Chamong Tee Exports, while narrating the story of his ancestor five generation removed, the enterprising pioneer of his company.

According to Lohia, Senai Ram had set out from his hometown in Ratangarh, Rajasthan and made his way to Dibrugarh in Assam, starting first with what he was best at: opening a grocery shop. His subsequent generations became landlords and indigenous bankers, offering finance under the *hundi* system. It was in exchange for an unrequited loan given to a local Assamese that the family acquired their first tea garden: Sewpur Tea Estate in 1916 in Tinsukia.

By the time of the 1881 census it is said that there were 2,400 Marwaris living in Assam. (Taknet: 2002; Based on the account in *The Heritage of Indian Tea*). Families like the Kanois, Jalans, Poddars, Goenkas, Birlas and Pauls were contributing significantly to its economy. Much later, they would buy over the jute and tea businesses in the land where they had once come to seek their fortune. This would largely be in the years just before the Second World War.

The Managing Agency Houses

Initially, it was the managing agency houses that flourished in Calcutta. With head offices in England, these agency houses had been set up mostly in partnership with former wealthy personnel of the East India Company. They managed commercial companies with interests in tea, besides commodities such as indigo, cotton, jute, coal and steel. The first such Agency House, a partnership by the name of Gillanders Arbuthnot, was established in 1819. After entering the tea business as garden agents, they became agents for the Darjeeling Himalayan Railway Co. Ltd in 1881.

Over the years, several managing agency houses like Macneill & Barry, Andrew Yule, Jardine Henderson, Shaw Wallace, Octavius Steel, Turner Morrison, Duncan, McLeod's, James Finlay, James Warren and Anderson Wright gained stature. Many of them, albeit with interchanging partnerships, flourished and stoked the tea business. For instance, Octavius Steel, a Scottish bachelor, disengaged himself from his partner A.R. McIntosh, to concentrate on tea gardens in Cachar, Sylhet and the Dooars.

Most firms as well as young planters who came out to India were, in fact, Scottish. It was boom time for tea in the 1870s, and the managing agency houses basked in inflated glory. However, with the turn of the century, as the Raj began to lose its shine, the shadows of decline fell on the Managing Agency House culture as well. In post-independent India, in 1956, government laws prohibited these managing agencies from controlling companies with voting stock without equity holdings in the company, as was the case so far. Devaluation in 1966 further added to their woes and many companies sent back their expatriate staff, as they were now called. Finally, in 1973, the curtain came down on the managing-agency system.

Meanwhile, many of the enterprising Marwaris had purchased the overseas holdings of the managing-agencies and bought over their Indian-based equity. Almost eighty per cent of the industry fell into their hands. The Indian tea industry had come into its own.

FACING PAGE ABOVE: AT&W Daniell Print showing Chowringhee, Kolkata as it was in 1798.
CENTRE: An archival engraving shows various aspects of making tea.
BELOW: Ashok Kumar Lohia, Chairman of the Kolkata-based Chamong Tee Exports narrates the story of his ancestors.

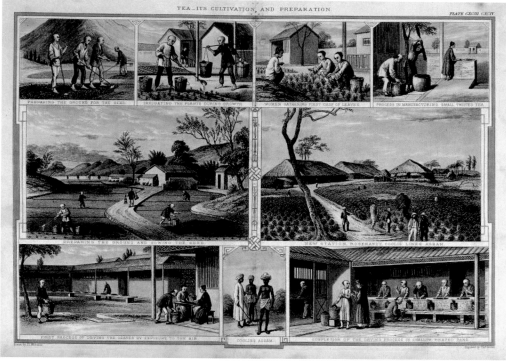

TEA—ITS CULTIVATION, AND PREPARATION

ABOVE: Some of the key players of the Indian Tea Industry.

FIRST ROW LEFT TO RIGHT: Dr K.K. Jajodia, Mr B.M. Khaitan, Mr Chirinjiv Bedi.

SECOND ROW LEFT TO RIGHT: Mr B.K. Birla, Mr Karan Paul, Mr Dikshit Arya.

CONTEMPORARY WORLD OF INDIAN TEA

'Tea is one of the mainstays of civilization in this country.'

~ *George Orwell*

As a testimony to its past, Kolkata continues to be the 'tea capital' of the country and most head offices of the large players of the tea industry are based in this city. The erstwhile managing agency houses have been reconstituted and incorporated under the Indian Companies Act. For instance, in the late 60s, Gillanders Arbuthnot & Co. Ltd (GACL) as it is now called, became part of the G.D. Kothari Group of Companies and deals in engineering, textiles, trading and tea. Like the earlier managing agency houses, large tea entrepreneurs have their foothold in other industries as well, even though tea is a significant component of their business activity. The passage of time, nevertheless, has reconfigured several of these tea companies.

> The original Assam Company, now Assam Company (India) Limited (ACL), for instance, has a later history that features Lord Inchcape, who had created an international business empire, together with acquiring extensive tea operations in India.

Ultimately the Macneill & Barry partnership emerged, and in 1949, three other merchant trading partnerships were amalgamated, of which their principals included the Assam Company. These became a subsidiary of the UK-based Duncan Macneill Group. In 1992, Dr K.K. Jajodia bought over the Inchcape holdings and the Company was rechristened to its present name, Assam Company Limited, of which he is Chairman, with his son Aditya Jajodia as Managing Director.

True to its generic profile, the Company's tea operations are concentrated only in Assam. It produces sixteen-seventeen million kilograms of tea annually, twenty-five per cent of which gets exported.

Other Major Players

The privilege of being the world's largest bulk tea producer today rests with the McLeod Russel–Williamson Magor Group. The history of this Group starts with Captain J.H. Williamson, who, in 1869, partnered with R.B. Magor, an assistant with the Great Eastern Hotel in Calcutta. In 1947, a young lad of nineteen, Brij Mohan Khaitan (known also as B.M.), presently Chairman of this Group, stood resolutely outside Hampton Court, a splendid office bungalow on a street lined with mango trees, daring himself to meet an intimidating senior of the managing agency house of Williamson Magor. He wanted to supply wooden chests for tea packaging.

By the time Williamson Magor became a limited company, in 1954, B.M. had started selling fertilisers to their tea estates, and had become a close friend of the founder's grandson, Pat Williamson. In 1963, he was asked to join the Board, eventually to become the Managing Director of the Group.

Hampton Court was redesigned to acquire its iconic address, 'Four Mangoe Lane'. Later came the merger of Williamson Magor with Macneill and Barry Ltd

of the Inchcape Group and the new company was renamed Macneill and Magor Limited. The coup d' triumph was the takeover of the Guthrie family's major stakeholding of the McLeod Russel Group in 1987. Next, it demerged from the Inchcape Group and today Williamson Magor's tea business functions as McLeod Russel India Limited.

The Company has extensive tea gardens in Assam and Dooars, producing over eighty million kilograms of tea annually, approximately a fifth of the entire tea production in Assam. Of this, thirty to thirty-three per cent is exported. Together with tea interests in Uganda, Rwanda and Vietnam, McLeod Russel produce almost 100 million kilograms of tea globally. B.M.'s sons Deepak and Aditya are now in the line of business.

Another strong player in the tea industry is Jay Shree Tea & Industries Limited. The historic Darjeeling Consolidated Tea Company Limited was brought within its fold in 2008. As a part of the well diversified conglomerate of the Birla Group, Jay Shree Tea accounts for nearly eleven per cent of the tea produced in Darjeeling. Tea is a personal passion for Chairman B.K. Birla, and this is the only company that has a presence in all the major tea-growing regions in the country. Its gardens in Upper Assam, Cachar, Dooars & Terai, Darjeeling and in South India together produce approximately twenty-four million kilograms of

tea annually. The company exports about seven million kilograms of tea annually and has also acquired tea estates in Uganda and Rwanda in Africa.

On the other hand, the long-standing Apeejay Surrendra Group under Chairman Karan Paul, focus their tea interests wholly in Assam. Formerly known as the Assam Frontier Tea Limited, and established in 1889 by A.R. Gordon Shaw in London, the company was taken over by the Apeejay Group in the eighties. It now directs operations through Apeejay Tea Limited, Empire & Singlo tea plantations and Kharjan Tea Estate, producing approximately twenty-five million kilograms of tea. Gardens like Sessa, Khobong and Pengaree produce teas that are exclusive.

Faint echoes of the bygone British era of tea in India still resonate in the international Goodricke Group Limited, headquartered at Camellia Plc., Linton Park in Kent, UK. The Group acquired its first tea garden in Assam, the Sephinjuri Bheel Tea Company in 1889. It then acquired a major shareholding in Walter Duncan & Goodricke Limited. Later, the company had a merger with the Balmer Lawrie Group and eventually came to be known as Camellia Investments Limited. The company's India

ABOVE: Runglee Rungliot is one of Duncan Industries Limited's reputed tea gardens that markets packaged tea by this name.
FACING PAGE: Sacks of premium tea ready for the market.

operations were incorporated in 1977. Goodricke Tea has a sizeable spread of tea gardens in Upper Assam, Dooars, Darjeeling as well as Kerala and Tamil Nadu that together produce about twenty-five million kilograms of tea.

Also steeped in history are the Duncan Industries Limited tea gardens that spread over Darjeeling, Dooars and Terai. In 1858 Walter Duncan, a young Scottish merchant came to Calcutta and established a partnership with Playfair to set up his managing agency house called 'Playfair Duncan'. Later, it was replaced by brother William and the firm of Duncan Brothers Limited continued to do well. In 1950, the agency houses of Duncan Brothers and Octavius Steel were bought over by the House of Goenkas. Of their multifarious family businesses, Duncan Industries with its tea division came under the chairmanship of G.P. Goenka. The Company produces close to sixteen million kilograms of tea.

In another reconfiguration, the well-known managing agency house established by James Warren in 1850 came to be incorporated in 1977 as Warren Tea Limited. Since 1983, it has been running as a successful family partnership concern with A.K. Ruia as Chairperson and Vinay Goenka and Vivek Goenka as Partner Directors. With an annual production of sixteen million kilograms of tea, Warren Tea is one of the largest bulk tea producers in India, and has plantations concentrated wholly in Upper Assam.

This is what the key players have to say on Tea:

Dr K.K. Jajodia, Chairman, Assam Company India Ltd: *'Opportunity responsiveness is our biggest strength.'*

Mr B.M. Khaitan, Chairman, Mcleod Russel (India) Ltd: *'Tea is not a mere commodity for us, it is a heritage, based on values and culture full of sentiments and commitments.'*

Mr B.K. Birla, Chairman, Jay Shree Tea & Industries Ltd: *'Perfection in a tea cup is what we achieve here at Jay Shree Tea.'*

Mr Karan Paul, Chairman, Apeejay Tea Ltd: *'My taste is evolving just like the Indian tea drinker …still there is nothing like a cup of strong Assam Single Estate Tea.'*

Mr Chirinjiv Bedi, Managing Director, Rossell Tea Ltd: *'At Rossell, quality is our creed. It is non-negotiable, it is consistent and it is a habit.…'*

Mr Dikshit Arya, Director, Aquarious Mktg Ltd: *'Merchant Tea Exporters have been pivotal to the development of the tea industry…opened new markets and led to innovations in packaging, and drinking habits.'*

In South India, The Bombay Burmah Trading Corporation now belongs to the eminent Parsi industrialist House of Nusli Wadia, under the Mudis Group of Estates. Their stronghold of tea estates in the Nilgiris and other parts of Tamil Nadu have an annual production of about eight million kilograms of tea.

Within the same region, the present day Amalgamations Group, dates back to 1858, when Robert Stanes landed in Madras at the tender age of seventeen, disconcerted at first, finding the place to be 'quite an ordeal and somewhat alarming.' Still, he did well enough to get into the tea business.

In 1922, Nilgiris Tea Estate Company Limited (now called United Nilgiris Tea Estates, UNTE) was formed and in 1960, the late S. Ananthramakrishnan, head of a prominent business conglomerate bought over the Stanes holdings that are now a part of this Group.

The claim for being the largest producer in South India rests with Harrisons Malayalam Limited, headquartered in Kochi. This company comes under the R.P. Sanjiv Goenka Group and has an annual tea production of twenty million kilograms.

Some of these large bulk and loose tea producers also have a market share in packaged tea. Duncan Industries packaged tea brands such as Runglee Rungliot, Shakti, Double Diamond, No.1 and Sargam, command a good position in the market. Goodricke Group's packaged teas like Margaret's Hope, Badamtam and Castleton are also well known.

Whereas Jay Shree Tea sells various brands under its umbrella 'Birla Tea', Apeejay Tea has labels like 'Mantra' and 'Mahamantra' in the retail space. The Company also acquired the Premier Foods UK tea business with its label Typhoo which includes fruit infusions and flavoured teas.

HUL & TGBL

However, two giant conglomerates, Hindustan Unilever (HUL) and Tata Global Beverages Limited (TGBL), with their combined strength account for almost forty per cent of the market share. Well rooted in history, both these companies now have a transnational complexion, their products touching the daily lives of people in more ways than one.

Headquartered in India's commercial city of Mumbai, HUL is a subsidiary of the Anglo-Dutch company Unilever, which has its head offices in the United Kingdom. In India, it was first established in 1933 as Lever Brothers India Limited and in 1956, was rechristened as Hindustan Lever Limited. After a series of mergers and acquisitions, the company flourishes today as Hindustan Unilever Limited (HUL).

Unilever's massive presence in the packaged tea business resulted from the international acquisition of two significant historical companies. The first was the takeover of Brooke Bond & Company that had been founded by the Lancashire-born Arthur Brooke in England, who, in 1869, set up his first shop 'Brooke, Bond & Company' in Manchester. Interestingly, there was never a 'Mr Bond'; Brooke merely liked the sound of the name. In India, Brooke Bond & Company India Limited was formed in 1912, after having swept the market with its brand name Red Label Tea. The company joined the Unilever fold in 1984. Another great acquisition was that of Lipton Tea in 1972, a company whose earliest links with India had been forged in 1898 by Thomas J. Lipton & Company.

In 1994 both companies merged to form Brooke Bond Lipton India Limited (BBLIL) and two years on, came under the HUL banner. Apart from premium black leaf teas under the Lipton Green Label and Yellow Label brand, the company also markets a large range of other varieties, in loose leaf, tea bags and ready-to-drink formats. Brands such as Brooke Bond Red Label, Brooke Bond Taj Mahal, 3 Roses, have been ever familiar in the Indian market while Taaza and A1 are popular in the second-tier market.

Equally well recognised, Tata Global Beverages Limited (TGBL), formerly known as Tata Tea, is a part of the Tata Group, and this is one of the oldest and largest conglomerates that broke ground in India. It was set up in the late nineteenth century by the son of a Parsi trader, Jamsetji Nusserwanji Tata. A brilliant entrepreneur, he started with his cotton trading business in Bombay and built up enough capital to be among the first Indians to buy shares in Octavius Steel's sterling tea gardens in eastern Cachar in the 1870s.

Meanwhile, Finlay Muir & Company, a branch of the Glasgow-based James Finlay & Company, had opened offices in Calcutta in 1870 with businesses in trading and textile mills. By 1901, the company had stepped into

the tea business, managing tea estates in Assam, Sylhet, Cachar, Dooars and Darjeeling, as well as the Kanan Devan Hills and Anamalai Hills estates in the south. In 1964, Tata created a joint venture alliance with James Finlay to form Tata Finlay. At this time, James Finlay and McLeod Russel owned equal holdings but later, this ownership structure of Finlay Tea Associates was redefined. In 1983, the combined equity was sold to Tata Finlay, and it was reconstituted as Tata Tea Limited.

Tata Tea made a thrust into the branded tea market in 1991, a move that would lead to the acquisition of the UK-based Tetley Group nine years later. The Company made further global imprints with acquisitions such as Eight O' Clock and Good Earth in the United States and Grand in Russia. The Company now goes by the name of Tata Global Beverages Ltd and is headquartered in the UK.

In India, Tata Global Beverages' packaged teas are household names. Besides their national brands, Tata Tea and Tata Tetley, the Company also has three regional brands—Kanan Devan, Chakra Gold and Gemini, each with their own market segment. As Tata Tea evolved into Tata Global Beverages, the Company made a landmark move for the industry in a decision to make the plantation workers owners of the enterprise by transferring control to an employee-owned private limited company. Similarly too, HUL has transferred its tea plantation business to its wholly-owned subsidiaries.

ABOVE: The managing agency house of the Williamson Magor partnership started in 1869, in a bungalow that stood in a mango-tree lined lane.

Besides the large corporate players, there are other known companies who have a weighty presence in packaged tea. One such name is the Wagh Bakri Tea Group. Its founder, Narandas Desai, who hailed from the western state of Gujarat, was known to be a follower of Gandhi in South Africa.

He set up a tea estate there in 1892, but racial discrimination forced him to return to India. His three sons took up the business in Ahmedabad, and the family set up Gujarat Tea Processors and Packers Ltd in 1980. Now headed by Chairman and Managing Director Piyush Desai, and with over thirty million kilograms of tea distribution, The Company has claims to be the third largest packaged tea company in India. The company has spread its wings to the broader domestic market, besides developing a reputed global outreach.

Some illustrious business houses in India's industrial landscape also maintain their stake in packaged tea brands, as in the case of Godfrey Phillips India of the K.K. Modi Group, who offer several selectively produced blends under 'Tea City', besides exporting speciality and bulk teas. Even as such brands extend their markets overseas, conversely, others like the UK-based international Twinings brand, recognising the vast potential in India, have established their own distribution network here as Twinings Pvt. Ltd. The Company has long standing repute in the category of premium tea bags and is ever familiar in the Indian retail trade.

Nevertheless, domestic brands like Golden Tips, Girnar, Infinitea, Gopaldhara, Sapat and several others do flourishing business. Besides, there are a host of local players that attract markets in satellite towns and villages. There is, then, a vast gamut of packaged tea brands that are popular, be it in urban supermarkets or in rural grocery shops across the country.

Tea Board of India

The vast and varied landscape of the tea industry qualifies it as an economic activity of national importance, and so it justifiably falls under the auspices of the Indian government. The Ministry of Commerce and Industry has therefore set up the Tea Board of India, a statutory organisation to protect and promote tea growers and producers and assist in the constant improvement of tea cultivation and the marketing of tea, both in the area of domestic and international trade.

> The genesis of this organisation dates back to 1903 when the Indian Tea Cess Bill was passed by the Viceroy, Lord Curzon, to tax tea to raise finances for marketing tea both within and outside India. The present Tea Board was set up under an Act in 1953, and formally constituted on April 1, 1954.

Members of the Board are drawn from a cross-section of Members of Parliament, tea producers, tea brokers, traders, consumers, representatives of governments from regional tea producing states and trade unions. It functions through various committees designated to look after its administration, export promotion, labour welfare for plantation workers, development for overseeing various new schemes floated by the Board and issuing of requisite licences. It has zonal, regional and sub-regional offices in the major tea producing areas, besides overseas offices in London, Dubai and Moscow.

To maintain and promote the image of tea, the Tea Board has created specially designed logos, an expressive representation of each region, to reflect the character and quality of its tea. This brand support system has been created to aid Indian exporters to market tea in packets that are of hundred per cent Indian origin and it can be used by them after complying with requirements for the logo usage. Effectively, all teas produced in India are administered by the Tea Board. In particular, protection of brand identity extends on a legal basis to Darjeeling tea that falls under the intellectual property rights of the word 'Darjeeling' and its logo on a world-wide basis.

In the words of Mr M.G.V.K. Bhanu (IAS), Chairman, Tea Board of India:

> 'Tea is not only a drink to cheer you up; it is good for health too. We at Tea Board of India believe in the saying – *Chai piyo, mast jiyo!* (Have tea and enjoy life).'

The Market Picture

The Indian tea market is always brewing with change, with large players either divesting or taking over plantations. The gardens continue to retain their original names, surviving the management reconfigurations brought about by the turning wheels of time. The companies mentioned herein are just a few vignettes of the past that lives on today.

The dynamics of the tea industry are further changing as small regional players have got a tremendous boost with the emergence of 'bought tea leaf factories' to whom they can sell their green leaf directly. It is, in fact, this huge and varied profile of tea producers that combine to give this country its sustained position as one of the world's largest producers of tea, next only to China (1761.00 million kg*) with an annual output of 1111.76 million kilograms*, which is more than twenty per cent of the entire world output of 4526.98 million kilograms* of tea.

FACING PAGE: Portrait of former prime minister Mrs Indira Gandhi in the office of Chairman, Tea Board of India. Her comment on the cup of tea is succinct.

What a difference a good cup of tea makes

Indira Gandhi

INTO THE
HEARTLANDS
OF TEA

Of all the tea aromas, however, there is none other than the fragrance of garden-fresh tea straight from the plantation, processed in its own factory. The beverage exhilarates with an added zest, in a world far removed from the urban clamour. In all likelihood you would be fascinated by the sheer spread of flat tea domains that stretch far into the horizon, as you sip your cup atop the sit-out of a Chang bungalow, if you happen to be in a tea estate in Assam. Whereas in any of the hill tea plantations of Darjeeling or South India, you may well be delighted by scenic vistas of tea bushes scaling the slopes in rhythmic unison. A large tea estate may extend over hundreds of hectares of land with rows of neatly configured tea bushes interspersed with geometrically spaced tall trees, planted to provide a uniform protection from wind and shade. An unmatched solace envelops the tea gardens, a silence that is only broken by the twitter of birds in the blush of a morning sky or the night-song of frogs and crickets under a canopy of brilliant stars.

FACING PAGE: The majestic Kanchenjunga provides a stunning backdrop to Darjeeling town in the Himalayan ranges. Prayer flags fluttering in the wind captivate the visitor.

ABOVE: Plucking never stops, rain or shine. A worker intent on her task despite the hot sun beating down her back.

PICTURESQUE TEA TOURISM

'Each cup of tea represents an imaginary voyage.'

~ *Catherine Douzel*

Indian teas, having taken seed in different regions, are endowed with a multitude of characters, each unmatched in their body, liquor and aroma. This vast repertoire arises from the volatile responses of the tea plant to its varying environment. As a result, with such a diverse geography and weather patterns, this sprawling land produces so many varieties of tea that it is a sort of Nature's Super Mall. Here one can opt for any category: delicate and pale or strong and dark, long leaf Orthodox or crushed and curled CTC, exclusive and expensive or accessible and cheap—there is a tea for every taste and inclination.

> The Assam lowlands, better known as the Surma and Barak Valley, produce teas with a profile that is entirely different from teas of the eastern Himalayan hills of Darjeeling. Both these regions are neighbours, but their scale and ethos is so unlike each other that their teas cannot be even regarded as cousins.

Then again the perennial harvest of the coastal mountains or ghats and the hills of South India yield teas that have neither the look nor the flavour of Darjeeling or Assam, but have special characteristics of their own.

These major tea belts, along with smaller pockets like the Terai, Dooars, Kangra Valley and the Kumaon Hills, not only offer the tea enthusiast a host of flavours, but also a great opportunity to visit a vast gamut of regions, each endowed with its own milieu, so that the Indian tea trail becomes a multidimensional experience. China as the global leader has a production that is largely green tea.

Beyond the Brew

Nowadays several tea planters have thrown open their bungalows to offer homestays. Drink in the flavours of history as these are heritage bungalows, where the bygone era of planters' lifestyle comes to the fore as you find yourself housed in enormous bedrooms that have old-fashioned armoires and winged dressing mirrors accompanied by equally capacious bathrooms. The living room will invariably have a fireplace and the dining table could be a heritage piece of burnished rosewood. The deferential staff offers impeccable service that includes the early morning cuppa. These commodious habitats were the outcome of a distinctive hybrid of architectural styles that the planters developed to combat the tropical heat, even as they tried to recreate a small piece of England for themselves while luxuriating in the vast expanse of space at their disposal.

In Assam, a unique kind of planter's residence came about to keep out wild animals and floods. It was raised on stilts made of steel that was shipped from England, and the etched markings, 'Made in Birmingham', can still be read on them today. Chang bungalows, as they were known, have an elevated veranda which extends into a covered deck. Here, relaxed, the British *burra sahib* or the 'big boss', who would sit in his planter's chair and get a bird's eye view of gardens, while enjoying the breeze that wafted through the stilts.

An exceptionally impressive version of a Chang bungalow can be found on Maijan Tea Estate of Assam Company Limited. Instead of stilts, this gracious bungalow is elevated on a pillared porch with a curving driveway and an expanse of garden green that overlooks the Dibru River. Originally, the bungalow is said to have been constructed around 1850 on a wooden plinth of four feet in height with a thatch roof. The bungalow was destroyed by a fire in 1885 and it took over four years to reconstruct it, this time with a more elaborate design, that had a grand living room and a spacious dining room on the ground floor, together with a small office for the superintendent on the western side of the Bungalow.

Around 1947, just before India's independence, these new trappings qualified this bungalow to be chosen as the venue for hosting a stay for members of the Royal Family, distantly related to Lord Inchcape and who were to visit the East India Company at Kolkata and the Assam Company's tea gardens. The hospitality was to include a grand banquet for the royal visitors. Hence the bungalow was further upgraded to adopt an imperial facade and its iron stilts were bricked and cement plastered from the base to the top-floor flooring to transform into the pillars. So exclusive and grand was the result, that it earned the name, 'White House'.

Most of the tea gardens have a story to tell, having acquired their name for a reason. Old English appellations like Assam Company Limited's Greenwood Tea Estate—so christened because of its lush environment—coexist with ethnic derivatives as in McLeod Russel India Limited's Sepon Tea Estate (in local dialect, *sia pan* means weave).

In Darjeeling, Makaibari Tea Estate acquired its name when, in 1835, Captain Samler with a handful of Gorkha sepoys decamped from a British military outpost and cleared a piece of land in the hills where they planted a patch of maize or *makai*, eventually to plant tea and bequeath the garden to the Banerjee family. Then again, the curiously English-sounding Margaret's Hope Tea Estate of the Goodricke Group was named after the daughter of its original owner, Mr Cruikshank. She is said to have fallen in love with the beauty of the estate and left for England, promising to return, but never did. She died of a tropical disease on board the ship and her father named the garden in her memory.

FACING PAGE: A smiling worker adds to the charm of a tea garden in Darjeeling.

ABOVE: White House, so named because of its gracious architecture, is an outstanding planter's bungalow at Assam Company Limited's Maijan Tea Estate.

OVERLEAF. A setting sun provides spectacular hues to a cloudy sky over a tea estate in Assam. Homestay on a tea plantation provides opportunities for splendid views that can be enjoyed over a cup of truly garden-fresh tea.

In South India too, there are mixed monikers like UNTE's Chamraj Tea Estate in the Nilgiris and Harrison Malayalam's Lockhart Tea Estate in Munnar. Tea towns around these gardens also resonate with history. There is, therefore, always the option to book yourself into a colonial style hotel in the vicinity, run by a savvy management.

Spend your evenings by the fireside of a bar, served by a wizened bearer who regales you with stories of his forefathers who served in the times of the sahibs. Enjoy a visit to an atmospheric planters' club. Top it up with a game of tennis or a round of golf in a scenic setting, just as the English planters did, in their leisure time. Assam alone boasts of twenty-one golf courses, most of them accredited to the tea plantations.

Many of the plantations skirt the banks of the mighty Brahmaputra, the 'Son of Lord Brahma, the Creator,' the second largest river in India. It is unique in being considered the only 'male' river in India, a country where rivers are always revered as *devis* or goddesses. And no doubt, its strength is voluminous. Originating as it does from the glaciers of Tibet, and fed by the melting Himalayan snows during spring, the river invariably floods, eroding the bushes and inundating them with its heavy clay soil.

Tea bushes by the Dibru River, an offshoot of the Brahmaputra river, bear the brunt of erosion at Rungagora Tea Estate, one of the pioneering gardens of Assam Company Limited.

Still, the British initially chose to plant tea along the north and south banks of the river as it provided a valuable system of transportation at a time when there were no railroads.

ABOVE: Guests enjoying a lavish breakfast at McLeod Russel's Sepon Tea Estate.
FACING PAGE: [CLOCKWISE FROM TOP]
Chang means *machan* or a high platform. Such bungalows kept the early planters safe from wild animals;
The 'White House' porch has a regal driveway that overlooks an arena of beautifully manicured lawns;
The planters' bungalow at Harrison Malayam's Pattumala Tea Estate.

Add to all this, the idyllic backdrop of waterfalls and lakes, meandering rivers and scenic trails that offer a therapeutic commune with the outdoors. Adventure sports like river rafting, fishing and horse riding are always at hand in these unsullied surroundings. Further thrills include sighting of wildlife and exotic flora in national parks and game sanctuaries that abound aplenty, as the plantations invariably lie in proximity to untamed jungle lands.

Then again, embellish this with the colourful palette of regional imprints as every tea district has its own nuance, and the brew from its leaf epitomises a distinct culture. Fascinating places of worship abound in the form of temples, churches, mosques and monasteries. Local homesteads produce charming handicrafts that are perfect for take-home memories. Rhythmic beats and the lilt of songs fill the air as ethnic festivals are celebrated with verve while local dance forms depict grace, evoking the gods, moods and seasons.

The immense diversity of the country lends a special soul to Indian tea. And so, the enthusiast who decides to travel the tea trail will enjoy experiences that go much beyond the beverage. There is more to Indian tea than just the perfect cup.

ABOVE: Two-thirds of the world's population of one-horned rhinoceros is found in the game sanctuaries of Assam.

BELOW: Tiger spotting is common in the jungles of Bengal, Dooars and Terai.

FACING PAGE: Assam Company Limited's Rungagora Tea Estate by the banks of the Dibru, the region where the first tea expedition met the Singpho chief.

ABOVE: The bright coppery toned Assam brew is a good pick-me-up, morning or evening.

FACING PAGE: Expanses of tea plantations spread around Dibrugarh, Assam being the largest contiguous tea growing region in the world.

BOUNTY OF ASSAM

'A nice cup of tea invariably means Indian tea.'

~ George Orwell

Considered by many as the Shangri-La of north-eastern India, Assam is home to the immense flatlands, native to the tea plant, growing perhaps from time immemorial. They are ensconced within the folds of the Himalayas, Mount Naga and Patkoi, bordering China, Mynamar and Bangladesh.

This is an ancient region, where the local tribes, the Ahoms, ruled its eastern parts for nearly 600 years. Around 1821, the neighbouring Burmese began to have expansionist intentions that threatened to reach the doorsteps of the East India Company. Then came the First Anglo-Burmese War after which the governance of this region fell under the British administrative province called the Bengal Presidency. Much later, during the early twentieth century, it was designated as a separate province, and post-independence, it became a state of the Indian Union.

Dibrugarh is considered the gateway of upper Assam, where the tea pioneers first ventured forth, in a bid to grow tea in India. This is now the single largest contiguous tea growing region in the world and is credited with almost fifty-one per cent of India's output of tea. A fact that is announced at the airport itself. As the road exits through tea gardens lining either side of the road, their stunted tree-like pruned bushes stand out like a signature on the visual tapestry of the drive upcountry.

Tea Country

Here lies the cradle of true tea countryside. Interspersed between roadside bazaars that line passing towns like Tinsukia, Dikom, Chabua and Panitola, there are 'bought tea leaf factories' that service a large number of small tea growers around this area. At Makum, a tea town in the uppermost extremity of Tinsukia District, there are factories that make tea machinery, mostly Chinese owned. Interestingly, there was a time when a large population from China emigrated here during the 1830s. Tea history also mentions that C.A. Bruce enlisted the help of Chinese tea makers. The word *makum* itself is Chinese, and it translates as 'meeting point' and it is here that roads from the three towns of Tinsukia, Digboi and Doomdooma in upper Assam converge.

> The entire region is interlinked by vast tea estates. Their gates bear the logos of well-known tea companies like McLeod Russel India Limited, Assam Company Limited, Rossell Tea Limited, Warren Tea Limited, Goodricke Group Limited and many more. In parts, a rail track runs parallel along the route, merging as it were, with life on the road. The British laid down these tracks that sometimes ended up at the very doorstep of the tea estates.

In this vast 'motherland of tea', districts like Darrang, Goalpara, Lakhimpur, Nowgong, Sibasagar, Cachar and Karbi also have voluminous tea plantations.

Sibasagar, the last capital of the Ahom kings who ruled Assam, known in the early years as Rangpur, is a three-hour drive from Dibrugarh. It was where the British set up the earliest tea plantations. This becomes evident from the archives in a report prepared by A. Mackenzie, the officiating Secretary to the Bengal government (cited in 'Papers regarding the Tea Industry in Assam': 1873)

> '... the plants (tea plants) were afterwards removed to Joypore, in the Seebsaugor district, and a garden established, which was sold to the Assam Company in 1840 ...'

Tocklai Experimental Station

History becomes palpable at the legendary Cinnamara Tea Estate that was set up by Maniram Dewan in 1850. Although it now spells a lost past and is not so well kept, it is better known for the Tocklai Experimental Station that occupies a part of its premises. Established in 1911, this is a charming colonial style building surrounded by old trees and beautiful gardens with an exotic lotus pond.

The Institute has sophisticated laboratories with a team of agro scientists who conduct constant research for soil improvements and quality enhancement of the tea plant. It takes pride in having achieved one of the greatest feats in tea history, that is, the development of TV1, the first ever clone for the propagation of the tea plant. It was initiated by Mrs A.C. Tunstall, wife of a scientist who was based here, who, like her husband, was also interested in botany. She collected seeds from various sources and on a specimen plot, developed the 'Mother Bush' from which, for the first time, the tea plant was grown from a cutting rather than a seed. Her experiment proved a success, and eventually three tea clones, TV1, TV2 and TV3 developed at Tocklai were released to the industry in 1949.

This path-breaking development marked the beginning of a revolution in clonal selection to create Assam hybrid varieties and the vegetative propagation of tea.

Since the 1960s, the Tea Research Association (TRA) has been managing Tocklai. It works as a co-operative research body, part-funded by the Council of Scientific and Industrial Research (CSIR) and the Tea Board of India. Its advisory network covers Assam, Cachar, Dooars, Darjeeling and Terai regions.

Assam tea now holds a very special place in the world's tea market. Guwahati, the capital of the state, is one of the largest centres for tea auctions in the world.

FACING PAGE: [CLOCKWISE FROM TOP]
The Tocklai Experimental Station in Jorhat is located in a majestic colonial building and is the oldest and the largest of its kind in the world; State-of-the-art laboratories conduct research and development on tea cultivation; Signboard of the TES; 'TV1' or the historic 'Mother Bush'.

Bold and Colourful Assam Tea

Assam is the single largest contiguous tea growing region in the world. Of a total land coverage of 579.35* thousand hectares of tea through the various regional tea belts of India, Assam alone has a coverage of 322.21 thousand* hectares and a whopping number of 65,422** tea estates that produce almost 51% of India's output— an estimated 581.26*million kilograms of tea.

Moreover, this region has the distinction of having its own indigenous variety of tea which comes from the hardy Camellia Assamica, rather than the Chinese variety, the Camellia Sinensis. It gives a character that is rich and malty, with a full-bodied bright liquor or colour. Teas from Assam are favoured by those who enjoy a strong cup, to which milk and sugar, if added, do not in any way submerge their strength or flavour.

Just as the different qualities and characters of wine are affected by a number of variables like changes in climate, the amount of rainfall or even the positioning of sun and shade, so too with tea. However, the distinguishing range of both Assam and Darjeeling teas have a complexity that goes even further than wine due to their unique attributes of flushes or cycles of growth. During these periods, the plant throws forth its shoots in quick succession and then retreats into 'dormancy', only to re-emerge after a period of two to three weeks, once again for the next flush to adopt a different flavour.

A single plant can produce three or four types of tea. Teas from this region are largely manufactured by the CTC or Crush-Tear-Curl method, although rolled and twisted long-leaf Assam tea produced by the Orthodox method always holds a special place amongst connoisseurs around the world.

Assam First Flush

These teas for example, Bamonpookri and Orangajuli, are picked from tea bushes that have just started putting forth the fresh new shoots and buds after the cold winter when there is little or no growth.

Commencing from late March, the first flush is plucked for eight to ten weeks. Such teas, being young, carry a hint of green in their appearance and have a strong fresh flavour with a taste that tends to linger in the mouth.

They usually find their way in blends and also do well as breakfast teas as their high tannin content is a good 'pick-me-up' and gives an energetic headstart for the day.

ABOVE: Bold and colourful Assam teas have bright, coppery tones.

Assam Second Flush

As the summer advances from mid-May to mid-July, the teas begin to acquire a matured taste and are considered to be in their prime. When brewed, they have a dark red liquor released from the infused leaf. This is accompanied by a rich aroma, with a strong body and a smooth, malty flavour. Heavy rains and constant humidity result in a prolific yield and almost seventy-five per cent of Assam teas are produced during this season. Premium teas such as Oaklands, Digullturung, Hajna, Thowra, Dikom, Moran, Sepon and Bukhial are well received in the international market.

Assam Autumn Flush

Gradually, as the weather gets cooler, the 'Autumnals' make their way into the market. By this time the ambient moisture in the soil after the prolonged rains goes into the shoot of the leaf and dilutes some of its flavours. So, once again these are preferable for making blends.

The Romance of Tea Estates

Several tea estates offer stays where one gets the opportunity of being able to visualise the drama of discovery of these vast flatlands that are the original home of Indian tea. Manoj Jalan, for instance, is a fifth generation planter who offers a charmingly refurbished authentic Chang bungalow for stay on his Mancotta Tea Estate on the outskirts of Dibrugarh.

Then again, in the tea town of Jorhat, the spell of Assam's tea inheritance can be captured at the period-style mansion, Thengal Manor or at the Banyan Grove bungalow at Gatoonga Tea Estate besides the Burra Sahib's Bungalow at Sangsua Tea Estate—all of which are managed by the Heritage North-east hospitality chain, under the umbrella of the B&A Limited. Headed by chairman H. P. Barooah, this company is a proud participant in the indigenous heritage of Assam tea, being incorporated in 1915 as Barasali Tea Estate Ltd, having acquired its present name at the turn of this millennium.

LEFT: The Assam tea leaf is harvested from late March as the First Flush begins after a winter dormancy of the bushes.
OVERLEAF: Women pluckers file through a tea garden in upper Assam. They mostly belong to the *Baaganiya* community and were brought in by early British planters from outlying areas.

A Taste of Assam

Located on the banks of the Brahmaputra, scenic Guwahati, the capital of Assam and a fast growing city, has several museums, parks and local places of worship, including the famous Kamakhya temple.

The countryside, in this region, is an expression of tropical beauty. Apart from the tea plantations, rustic village homes with bamboo fences besides patches of emerald paddy fields, give way to local bazaars. Deciduous trees, picturesque bamboo groves, banana groves and coconut and areca nut palms add to the luxurious landscape.

The natural beauty of Jorhat, an important city on the tea map, manifests itself in its outskirts at Majuli, the largest river island in the world set in the Brahmaputra.

Wild life and birds enthral at the Dibru-Saikhova National Park north of Tinsukia. Also notable, are national parks like Manas and Kaziranga that have been recognised as World Heritage Sites. The latter has the distinction of being home to two-thirds of the world's population of the one-horned rhinoceros.

In this region too, lies the city of Digboi, the area known for its oil reserves. The saga of oil discovery gets linked with the discovery of tea. It is said that in 1828, while trying to reach Singpho territory, C.A. Bruce came across several oil seepages upstream of Makum. Around 1867, some engineers from the Assam Railway and Trading Company found their elephants' legs soaked in black mud, glistening with oil. They excitedly told their labourers to 'Dig-boy-dig!' and the name Digboi came to stay. The town has the world's oldest operating oil machinery and an oil museum, besides having a modern oil refinery.

The lush setting of this area provides the perfect backdrop for two golf clubs, the Digboi Golf Club and the Margherita Golf Club. The cottage industry of sericulture flourishes in Assam and many a village home has its own loom.

LEFT: Workers at Chamong Tee Export's Maud Tea Estate in Assam protect themselves from the heat by wearing typical *jaapi* hats from folded palm and bamboo leaves that grow abundantly in the tropical countryside.

Elsewhere, vistas of tea continue to spread around the countryside. The State, recognising its bountiful asset, organises an annual Tea Tourism Festival in Jorhat during November.

A 'must' during the celebrations is the *jhumar* dance, which the workers perform in *basti*s or plantation villages to celebrate any occasion.

For the festival of Bihu, held three times a year, in mid-January, mid-April and mid-October, the dances are more elaborate.

The women clad themselves in beautiful silk saris, typically in natural colours edged with red and black Assamese border weaves. The men wear *dhotis* and sometimes tie a similar cloth or a *gamchha* around their head.

The Assamese create many a reason for revelry. Perhaps it is because of the heady *tamul* (the raw areca nut that grows in abundance) partaken wrapped in betel leaves and offered as a mark of hospitality to guests after a meal and also after tea. Or perhaps it is the sylvan surroundings of the lush environs that fill them with a certain ebullience. This is a land with zest, just like its hearty teas.

FACING PAGE: [ABOVE] The males dance with abandon to the beat of a *dhol* and sounds of a *pepa*, a local flute. Folk dances in Assam, as in the rest of India, are usually communal in nature and are performed outdoors. [BELOW] Enraptured children watch the Bihu dance in a local community centre.
ABOVE: Girls sway with graceful hip movements as they perform to celebrate 'Bihu'.

ABOVE: Darjeeling teas release a light liquor when brewed and each variety has its own inimitable character. Their production is always long leaf Orthodox.

DIVINE BOON OF DARJEELING

'O Tea! O leaves torn from the sacred bough!
O stalk! Gift born of the great gods!
what joyful region bore thee …?'

~ *Pierre Daniel Huet*

The small and exclusive tea region around Darjeeling in the state of West Bengal is a jewel in the Indian treasure chest of tea. It spreads over the crests and slopes of the Phalut ridge of mountains that border Nepal and India. Endowed with a quaint celluloid beauty, the town itself is perched at a height of 2134 metres above sea level and it derives its name from the word *Dorje Ling* or, Abode of the Thunderbolt, which came from the mythological sceptre of Lord Indra, the God of Rain. True enough, the region is often overcome by whimsical clouds that give rise to frequent rain showers. From this constant humidity and the unique acidic soil character of its hills, emerge some of the world's most celebrated teas.

The exclusivity of Darjeeling tea has earned it the distinction of being the first product in India to be accredited with a Geographical Indication (GI) status. By this, no other tea may be permitted to be labelled 'Darjeeling', just as no other wine in the world be labelled 'Champagne', unless produced in the Champagne district of France, or no other whiskey in the world may be labelled 'Scotch' unless it is actually produced in Scotland, or no other tangy cheese may be termed 'Cheddar' unless it has been produced in the Cheddar district of England.

Such a mandate of the GI notification is accorded by the World Intellectual Property Organisation to 'goods that have a specific geographical origin and which possess qualities or a reputation that is due to that place of origin.'

Flavourful Darjeeling Tea

As compared to Assam, this region only has an estimated production of 9.02 million kilograms of tea* a year, accounting for just about one per cent of all of India's teas. Moreover, with a niche land acreage of an estimated 17, 818 hectares**, it has only 85** tea gardens that are sprinkled within Darjeeling district which includes the areas around Kurseong, Sadar Division and Kalimpong.

Darjeeling teas are invariably Orthodox, and their distinction is enhanced by the seasonal patterns that are even more pronounced than those of Assam. Then again, these are further influenced by the varying altitudes of the tea gardens and the individual exposure of the slopes to sun and rain. The cyclic flushes therefore create a host of subtle characters.

The tea bushes that grow in these parts provide a liquor or a beverage that is light and delicate in colour, flavour and aroma. Their distinguishing qualities remain an enigma. Many experts claim that were this variety of tea to be planted anywhere else in the world, the Darjeeling taste would never be replicated. Experiments have been conducted by the Tea Research Association in India to explore this phenomenon.

When a Darjeeling tea plant was taken to similar mountain regions in Himachal Pradesh, it failed to produce the typical Darjeeling flavour. Conversely, when Nilgiri tea plants from the hills of South India were grown in Darjeeling, their yield changed,

giving rise to the same inimitable Darjeeling tea character. Ashok Lohia of the Chamong Group rates this tea 'a miracle'. He speculates that it could be the *terroir*, or a combination of soil and latitude, or perhaps the ultra violet rays of the sun that give it a pinkish sheen—flavours that cannot be matched anywhere else in the world.'

The tea is all the more coveted because of its limited production. Most of the bushes belong to the original Chinese strain, the Camellia Sinensis, a variety that is more delicate and slow growing compared to the resilient Camellia Assamica. Some may, in fact, belong to the original plantings and be over 150 years old. The cold climate also inhibits the output of the bushes. With winter snow, they are blanketed into dormancy. In its physical attributes, the Darjeeling leaf is smaller

and lighter in weight, and therefore involves a stronger withering process during production. More plucking would be required to produce a batch of tea of the same quantity as Assam tea. Plucking is laborious, as the craggy terrain makes it difficult for workers to navigate through the bushes. As a result, productivity per hectare of Darjeeling tea is only one-third of that in Assam. So small and exclusive is the yield that only one per cent of India's tea comes from this region. This tea therefore commands a higher price in the market.

ABOVE: Picture-postcard Darjeeling sits atop craggy Himalayan ranges that crown a tropical latitude. With seasonal changes and scuttling clouds that give frequent rain showers, the extraordinary geography of this region results in producing teas with flavours that remain unparalleled in the world.

Darjeeling First Flush

These greenish-brown teas come from the new shoots that are harvested from mid-March to April. Compared by some to new Beaujolais wines, they come after a long wait, once the winter moderates. As the fresh young stems have just emerged from dormancy, the quantity produced is limited. First Flush teas are considered among the finest and are therefore much in demand. They produce a cup that is very light in colour with a floral character and a slightly sharp taste, and are best taken without milk. They are well-loved in Japan, Europe and America where much of this variety is exported.

ABOVE: Located in Kalimpong, Teesta Valley Tea Estate has a history of fine tea, having been established in 1841.

Darjeeling Second Flush

These teas are picked between May and June and are also considered excellent. They are more full-bodied as the growth is more vigorous by this time. They are brighter in liquor and have a fruity note, with a better keeping quality and do well as afternoon or evening tea.

Muscatel

For just about two weeks within the Second Flush each year, come the Muscatel teas, with flavours unrivalled and evocative of Muscat grapes. This is the time when Nature entices aphids or green flies that breed for a short spell to enjoy the sap of the leaves and chew on them. The leaf gets bruised, inducing an enzyme

FACING PAGE: Workers pluck the enigmatic Darjeeling leaf.
ABOVE: Nathmull's Company was set up in 1931 by the migrant Sarda family from Rajasthan who settled in Darjeeling and took to marketing tea.

reaction and its water content also gets reduced. As a result the stem becomes turgid and purplish in colour, with an inhibited growth that gives it a concentrated aroma.

Only the right combination of geographical conditions and careful processing in the factory can result in a small batch of tea qualifying to be called Muscatel.

The leaf is darker brown and may contain some silvery tip which results from the fine downy buds that are plucked along with the leaves.

In taste, it may be described as 'fruity' and sometimes, 'peachy,' and most tea lovers, especially in Europe, like to enjoy it with special varieties of cream and sugar.

Darjeeling Monsoon Flush

These are picked during the heavy rains between July and September. High moisture content results in teas that are darkest in colour, with the least bouquet, so they find utility in blends and tea bags.

Darjeeling Autumnal Flush

Teas harvested from October to November come under this description. They consist of large leaves that yield a coppery liquor and they have a stronger full-bodied taste as compared to monsoon teas.

FACING PAGE It is not uncommon to see school children winding their way through paths that traverse the tea gardens. A number of Scottish missionary and Anglo-Indian schools were set up as the British planters settled down in Darjeeling and some well-known heritage educational institutions exist even today.

OVERLEAF: At the Batasia Loop, against the canvas of the Himalayan ranges, the narrow gauge tracks form a unique turnaround after which the toy train makes its descent into the town.

ABOVE: Pluckers navigate the steep terrain under blue summer skies and warm sunshine.

FACING PAGE: A tourist does an amateur tea tasting at Makaibari Tea Estate.

The Romance of Tea Estates

The picture postcard town of Darjeeling has its nearest airport at Bagdogra, ninety kilometres away. If one decides to fly in, the road journey from this touch point to the tea estates in this charming district is an experience to cherish as the countryside reveals a fascinating mix of Himalayan beauty and sub-tropical vegetation. Amidst this setting, the wonderland of tea unfolds over hills and slopes ranging from elevations as low as 100 meters and going up to 2000 meters above sea level.

In the lower heights, the climb goes through a tangle of greenery giving way to thick deciduous forests. Wild flowers and gigantic ferns cascade forth from the hill faces. Higher up and closer to Darjeeling town, moss covered fir, spruce and birch trees reach skywards in the bracing air. Come summer, and the flitting clouds reveal visions of snow-clad peaks that provide a theatrical backdrop for the rows of tea bushes that flow along the sharply contoured mountainsides, plunging through sharp valleys into the lap of crystal streams.

Kurseong, an area that produces some of the finest teas in the district, is on this road route. Amongst its well-known tea gardens is Swaraj Kumar aka 'Rajah' Banerjee's forested Makaibari Tea Estate, famed for its organic black and green teas, besides its production of specialised limited quantities of 'white' tea, coveted by connoisseurs.

While the estate's well-appointed bungalow, Stone Lodge, offers accommodation, this fourth generation planter, in his passionate commitment to the cause of the environment of which tea is integral, has further developed the concept of 'homestays'. He has assisted his garden workers to set up facilities in their village homesteads where visitors can stay and enjoy the true tea experience.

The Kurseong road traverses Goodricke Group Limited's Castleton Tea Estate, which is also skirted by the train line. This is one amongst eight tea gardens

that are in the Group's portfolio. With a market share in the packaged tea segment, some of their gardens have quaint-looking tea shops that sell their brands.

In this district too, is the Kejriwal family's highly reputed Jungpana Tea Estate. It adjoins Ashok Kumar's Goomtee Tea Estate that has a plantation bungalow set amidst a landscape that is bejewelled with colourful flora.

Here, guests can enjoy the ethereal sunrise over the mountains and sip the delicate Muscatel tea that grows deep within the folds of its picturesque valley that is threaded by six waterfalls and a warbling river bed. Closer to Darjeeling, in the sun-kissed Golden Valley

in Ghum district, the Chamong Group's Tumsong Tea Estate has 'Chai Bari', a delightfully resurrected bungalow where one enjoys tea while overlooking the twinkling lights of the town.

The Company has thirteen more tea gardens that are spread over areas of Rongbong Valley, Lebong Valley and the Teesta Valley.

Three kilometres below the town, a steeply winding road leads to Sanjay Bansal's Happy Valley Tea Estate of the Ambootia Tea Group. Like its name, the garden delights visitors by allowing them to clamber through the gardens and pick the leaf. Its tea factory is also open

to tours. Further up the road, little tea shops do brisk business selling packages of famed 'Darjeeling tea', so that this scenic point becomes a 'must-do' tourist spot.

Moving on to Kalimpong district, the Lopchu and Pashok tea gardens have earned their name. The former blazed a trail by being the first to market packets of Darjeeling tea. The Sikkim road runs through this region, with the river Teesta forming its northern boundary. Along the same stretch and by the river Rangeet, the Prakash family's Glenburn Tea Estate has a planter's bungalow that has been converted into a luxurious boutique hotel. Both these rivers also mark this district's eastern frontier with Bhutan. while Nepal lies to the North.

PAGES 96–97: An ethereal sunrise over Mt. Kanchenjunga. It rises amongst surrounding four peaks as a fifth jewel, its name translating into 'The Five Treasures of Snow'.

FACING PAGE: Established in 1868, the Darjeeling Planters' Club was considered the epitome of high society. Its land was donated by the Maharaja of Cooch Behar who earned the privilege of being the only person to be allowed to park his rickshaw in the main porch of the Club.

ABOVE: [CLOCKWISE FROM LEFT]
A print of a hill tribesman; The beautifully adorned Yiga Choling Monastery is the largest of the three monasteries in Ghum;
Sherpa Tenzing Norgay is Darjeeling's pride.

A Taste of Darjeeling

During the mid-nineteenth century, the town of Darjeeling developed rapidly with the success of tea. The British planters began to make churches and schools to facilitate a good life for their families and the memsahibs also favoured it as a good getaway from the sweltering summer of Calcutta, where their husbands were stationed.

With the flourishing of the tea business, transportation also improved. Although by 1878 a broad gauge railway line connected Calcutta to Siliguri, the rest of the stretch to Darjeeling was only negotiable by horse or tonga on a cart road. Francis Prestage, an agent of the Eastern Bengal Railway Company, put forth a proposal to the Lieutenant Governor of Bengal, Sir Ashley Eden, for connecting Siliguri to Darjeeling with a steam tramway. His design for a narrow gauge locomotive, the first of its kind, gained easy approval and the train was ready to make its maiden journey from Siliguri to Darjeeling on July 4, 1881.

Designated as a World Heritage Site by UNESCO, this toy train, as it is nicknamed, is a fascinating joy ride, besides serving its purpose as a means of transport. It commences its journey from New Jalpaiguri and chugs tenaciously through the steep mountainside without the aid of cogwheels at an unhurried pace of ten-fifteen kilometres per hour. It passes through townships with tracks criss-crossing the streets, almost like those of a tramline. It is easily possible to jump off, take a photograph, or go and chat with the local shopkeeper and re-board the train again. It climbs up to Ghum, the highest station in India at 2257.65 metres and starts the descent to Darjeeling town, going around the scenic Batasia Loop. At the Batasia Loop, against the canvas of the Himalayas, the narrow gauge tracks form a unique turn around after which the toy train makes its descent into the town. The War Memorial at the centre commemorates the local Gurkha martyrs who participated in the war operations that have taken place since independence.

This charming town could well be the pearl of the Eastern Himalayas. From its vantage point, one can get some mesmerising views of Mt Kanchenjunga, the third highest peak in the world. Its imposing snow-clad south face is best seen from Tiger Hill at sunrise. Sips of hot tea combat the early morning chill as the first glow of the sun on its shadowy summit unveils a spectacle so ethereal that the audience cannot help but break into an applause. Although it appears so close, the mountain lies on the eastern Nepal border.

These majestic views also remind one that Darjeeling is the homeland of the famous mountaineering tribe, the Sherpas, the kinsmen of the late Tenzing Norgay who accompanied Sir Edmund Hillary on the first ever conquest of Mt Everest. Himalayan Mountaineering Institute with its museum honours his memory and offers world class courses. The musuem and tea shop is a 'must' for a visitor.

The silence and calm of this mystic Himalayan world is also expressed in monasteries like the Yiga Choling and Ghoom Monastery that are bright in celestial hues. From neighbouring Nepal came the Gorkhas, who the British had begun to enlist as mercenaries in recognition of their courage and capacity for hard work, and who were also used by the planters as a labour pool for their tea gardens. The ethnic groups of this region have archetypal hill features, with rosy cheeks, broad faces and narrow eyes. The Gorkhas make up the majority,

FACING PAGE: At 2257.65 metres above sea level, Ghum is the highest railway station in India.

ABOVE: The Anglican Church of St. Andrew's is a landmark that dates back to 1843. Its early worshippers were Scottish soldiers and tea planters.

The heart of the town is Chowrastha, with its tourist-oriented shops. Besides, it has some charming heritage places of stay like the nineteenth-century ITC WelcomHeritage Windermere Hotel and the New Elgin Hotel both strongly reminiscent of the British era. Other landmarks are Glenary's, where one enjoys a cup of tea and cakes in an old-world atmosphere, while taking in beautiful valley-views through paned windows. Another attraction is Nathmulls Tea Shop of the Sarda family who have been in the business of selling tea for eighty years.

Darjeeling then, has a soft glow of history that lends it a sense of romance. Combined with the panorama of its scenic glory, it bestows the traveller with never-to-be forgotten memories. Images of lush mountain slopes amidst flitting clouds continue to linger in the mind, just like the distinctive flavours of its teas.

RIGHT: The Darjeeling Himalayan Railway or the 'toy train' as it is popularly called chugs past tea gardens. It is designated as a World Heritage Site by the UNESCO

BONANZA OF SOUTH INDIA

'There is a subtle charm in the taste of tea which makes it irresistible and capable of idealisation.'

~ Okakura Kakuzo

Home to the tea regions of South India, the Nilgiris and the coastal Western Ghats have a disposition far different from those of the Himalayas. Here, in these hilly heights with a subtropical setting, where winters are not too severe and humidity is stoked by two cycles of rainfall—the south-westerly monsoon as well as the north-easterly monsoon—the tea bushes experience no seasonal flushes and flourish throughout the year.

Teas from the South prevail with keynotes of their own. In hues of red-gold, they are crisp with neither the colour and strong body of Assam teas nor the pale delicacy of the Darjeeling varieties. Their character is something in-between. They are vigorous enough to make good breakfast teas. Yet their neutral liquors, subtle flavours and aromas make them pleasing for afternoon teas as well. Nilgiri tea from Tamil Nadu is crisp and clear and as it does not cloud, it is perfect for making iced tea. It can be enjoyed with or without milk. Teas from Kerala and Karnataka, on the other hand, have more coppery overtones.

In a general perspective, the entire region produces teas that are identified by their good colour and body, and are considered favourable for making blends. Besides, they balance the commercial economics of the product as they are priced lower due to their perennial production. They are therefore sought after by several brand companies, so that more than fifty per cent of the teas from this region are exported.

Aromatic Teas from the South

Although most of the teas are CTC, gardens in the higher elevations also produce some good Orthodox varieties that are well regarded internationally. Some of the finest teas come during the cold weather, being known as 'winter' or 'frost' teas. As temperatures fall, the growth of the bushes slows down so that the leaf conserves its flavours. Altitudes in the south, range from the high Nilgiris to undulating ghats and forested valleys, giving rise to an immense bio-diversity. Consequently, these teas reveal themselves in several distinct attributes, each region making a specific statement for its own quality of tea.

As compared to the north-east, tea gardens in the Nilgiris are relatively small, mostly averaging 100–200 hectares. There are an estimated 45,000 small holders who cultivate up to four acres of tea. To service this perennial and plentiful yield, there are more than 350 tea factories in this region Together, this adds up to a plentiful produce, running into millions of kilograms of tea that is sold every week at the Coonoor auction centre.

Thanks to the generosity of two monsoon spells, the tea bushes in this region experience no seasonal flushes and flourish throughout the year. Spreading over the states of Tamil Nadu, Kerala and parts of Karnataka, this region has the highest yield in the country, possibly in the world. Together, it contributes twenty-two per cent of India's total output that translates into an estimated

FACING PAGE: Visited frequently by misty clouds on undulating slopes, unhindered tea gardens add to the charm of Munnar tea country.

229.87 million kg* of tea. There are approximately 73,964** tea estates of which 68,374** tea estates lie in Tamil Nadu alone and these produce the largest share, the major yield coming from the Nilgiris. Next, Kerala, with its 5,557** tea estates has an impressive tea profile in South India. Although coffee predominates in Karnataka, it has 33** tea estates, that make a significant contribution to the country's basket of annual tea output. The combined production from these states therefore is of great value to the country's profile of teas. Due to its bio-diversity and varying elevations, South India produces several characters of tea that range from strong to light, being generally bright in colour and possessing a pleasing aroma.

Teas from Ooty

The drive through Kotagiri, a little tea town on the way to Ooty, establishes the supremacy of the Nilgiris as a tea district with vistas of tea gardens punctuated with eucalyptus trees that make up the countryside. Gentle elevations at approximately 1200 metres above sea level give rise to teas that are dark and strong. Further up, the teas get lighter and more flowery as they hint the Chinese strain of tea seed. The United Nilgiri Tea Estate Company Ltd (UNTE) of the Amalgamations Group produces high quality long leafed Orthodox tea at its Chamraj Tea Estate.

At 1650 meters, this estate overlooks tea gardens through magnificent misty views. Still further, the Group's Korakundah Organic Tea Estate at 2414 meters is the highest in South India, said to be the first of its kind in the world at such an elevation. In this quiet isolation, bison and elephants roam freely amidst forests of indigenous Shola trees. It is chequered with tree belts that give protection to the bushes from high velocity winds.

Teas from Coonoor

In the equally picturesque twin town of Coonoor, exist some of the oldest tea estates. Amongst these, the Mudis Group owns the historic Dunsdale Tea Estate with its high elevation gardens that produce quality Orthodox

LEFT: The colourful culture of the State of Tamil Nadu is reflected in its brightly hued village townships that have developed around the tea gardens. Each region in South India bears its own hallmark.

tea. Another known producer of fine teas is Nonsuch Tea Estate, dating back to the late 1800s. It qualifies to be amongst the official suppliers to the 'President's Household, Rashtrapati Bhawan of India.' The Thiashola Plantations Private Ltd, also a heritage tea estate, is known particularly for its organic teas. It is said that the British used Chinese prisoners of war to first plant tea here. Coonoor is the headquarters of the United Planters Association of Southern India (UPASI) a body that represents and protects the interests of planters in South India, besides conducting research in tea. Also housed here are the southern headquarters of the Tea Board of India.

Teas from the Anamalais

The tea trail in the Nilgiris continues through Coimbatore district with lower elevations ranging from 900–1600 metres that run between Tamil Nadu and Kerala. This is a land of thick rainforests, where the town of Chinnakallar receives the second highest rainfall in India. In 1857, pioneers like Carver Marsh and C.R.T. Congreve first braved these jungles to plant coffee which was replaced by tea plantations in the early twentieth century. Today companies like the Woodbriar Group, the Mudis Group and Jay Shree Tea & Industries Ltd of the B.K. Birla Group have their presence here. Bordering the two states, the town of Valparai is the tea hub where UPASI has a Tea Research Station. Teas from this area can be strong, zesty and fairly bright to make a good morning cup.

Wayanad & Nelliyampathy Tea

To the west of the Kundah range of the Nilgiri hills, just before the steep descent into the Malabar Coast is the district of Wayanad, a stretch of deep undulating jungle that lies in the state of Kerala.

As in most of South India, the initial plantations here too, were of coffee, pioneered by James Ochterlony in 1845, and these were later struck by blight. Then came the gold rush that attracted adventurers, which also soon died out. Finally, in 1887, the Wentworth Gold Mining Company was converted to produce what they found much more lucrative—tea. Several others followed suit.

RIGHT: Wild flowers exult in the moist mist of rain clouds that flit through the hill slopes.

Among the tea companies that operate here are those of the Woodbriar Group, the Mudis Group and the B.K. Birla Group. The Wentworth Tea Estate is now one of the holdings of the R.P. Sanjiv Goenka Group's Harrisons Malayalam Limited. Teas produced here are full-bodied, but with mild and mellow flavours.

South of the Palghat Gap in Nilgiris, lies Nelliyampathy, a small tea plantation district in Kerala. It does, however, have a few exclusive tea estates such as Manaluru of the A.V. Thomas Group, another well-established tea group in the south. Also of repute is Poabs Organic Estate that grows wholly organic tea. It was once known as the Seethargundu coffee estate, and dates back to 1889. This region has medium-range elevations that result in teas with a good flavour and body.

ABOVE: The Nilgiris offer a vista of tall trees and lush vegetation surrounding the terraced tea gardens.

Teas from Idukki District

This district can be considered the heart of Kerala and the tea trail commences with the port city of Kochi, erstwhile Cochin, which has the nearest airport.

Fort Kochy, the old town, still exhibits a splendid imagery of the past. This was the centre from where ships set sail with their cargo of tea despatched from the Madras Presidency. Today, tea companies like Harrisons Malayalam Limited have their headquarters

here and the city is also the largest centre for tea auctions in the south.

Peermedu, not far from Kottayam, was formerly the summer palace of the Maharaja of Travancore. It was here that J.D. Munroe first grew coffee in 1862. Tea plantations gradually developed in this area, with little towns like Kumily, on the coming up outskirts of Periyar Wild Life Sanctuary and Vandiperiyar.

Further west is *Pattumala*, or 'hill draped in silk', where tea plantations spread over the undulating expanses of low elevation hills criss-crossed with little streams. Two well-known tea companies that have their presence here are Harrisons Malayalam and A.V. Thomas & Co. They produce teas with a medium fragrance and a reddish liquor that do well for the mid-morning or afternoon cup.

Teas from Munnar

Munnar is really the quintessential tea town of Idukki district, nestling in the High Range or the Kanan Devan Hills. Here lies some of the highest parts of Kerala's Western Ghats, with Anamudi at 2695 meters towering as the tallest peak in South India. It was in 1877 that the then Cardamom Superintendent J.D. Munroe obtained the first 'pooniat' concession from the local Poonjar chief, and subsequently the Kanan Devan land concession. He was later joined by the Turner Brothers to begin the cultivation of cinchona. The first tea was planted here in 1880 in what is now known as Sevenmalley Tea Estate.

The hills around Munnar unfurl a splendour of uninhibited tea gardens spreading over rolling hills, with bushes that clamber to meet the curving roads. Amidst the vistas of tea, giant boulders sit silhouetted against the sky, reminiscent of the volcanic origins of the region. The town is the stronghold of the Kanan Devan Hills Plantation Company (P) Ltd.

KDHP succeeded Tata Tea in 2005, when the latter divested stake in its plantations in Munnar. Here, on the Nallathani Tea Estate, with its tea factory and museum, the curtain of the past lifts as accounts of the pioneering planters' several hardships come to light. One such story tells of their lonely lives, when so desperate were they to ensure business for the newly-set up post office, that they bought stamps and posted letters to themselves. Today, the KDHP Planters' Club is a well preserved vintage property, proud of its past. The KDHP Company's Tea Museum has memorabilia that recalls early planters' lives and displays old tea equipment. It also has a burial urn dating back to the second century BC, establishing the antiquity of this region.

RIGHT: Picturesque Wallardie Tea Estate of Harrisons Malayalam Group produces quality tea with a medium fragrance.

A few other tea companies such as the Woodbriars Group and Harrisons Malayalam also have their gardens here. The latter produce Orthodox tea at Lockhart and Panniar tea estates besides CTC tea at Surianalle Tea Estate. Most of these teas are strong and full-bodied, with an orange-gold liquor and a flavour that has a slightly fruity hint.

Teas from the High Wavys

Near the ancient and famed Meenakshi Temple of Madurai, deep in the steeply layered hills of the Meghamalai district, the Woodbriars Group owns the High Wavys Tea Plantation. Manalaar and Cloudlands are the other tea estates here. Tea ventures took root relatively late—during the early twentieth century—in these southern-most parts, hence gardens in this region qualify as among the highest yielding tea estates in the world. Further south, in the Tirunelveli district the Singampatti Group, another company of the Mudis Group have three tea estates, Manjolai, Manimutharu and Oothu, the last mentioned producing entirely organic tea. As the erstwhile Bombay Burmah Trading Corporation, this company had its beginnings in timber and came into tea much later.

ABOVE: Tea workers in the South remain busy throughout the year as the growth is perennial and there are no seasonal flushes.

Teas from Chikmagalur

Some teas with pleasingly balanced and medium characters grow around the town of Chikmagalur that is set amidst the Budan Giri Hills of the Western Ghats in the state of Karnataka. This however is predominantly a coffee growing district. Kelagur Coffee & Tea Estates, for instance, was first started as the Mysore Coffee Company around 1857. It was acquired by Diwan Bahadur S. L. Mathais, a reputed personality of his times, in 1927. It is now run by the fourth generation planter, Peter Mathais. Once again, being relatively 'young', these gardens are known for their exceptionally high yield and they produce high quality CTC teas, besides their production of well-known strains of coffee. The tea district also extends to nearby Hassan, sixty kilometres away.

Teas from Coorg

Set as they are, amidst predominantly coffee planting areas of Karnataka, these small tea belts in Coorg or Kodagu produce over 5000 kilograms of tea annually and find a relevant place on India's tea map.

Together, all these teas from the south make up a multitudinous variety of characters due to variations of elevations, climate and soil that occur across this region.

ABOVE: [CLOCKWISE FROM TOP LEFT]
The Kanan Devan Hills Plantation Company's Tea Museum set against the backdrop of the Nallathani Tea Estate;
Built in 1909, the Planters' Club in Munnar takes pride in its traditions;
Treats in the countryside. A friendly elephant enjoys being bathed by his handlers.

The Romance of Tea Estates

While there are several hotels and resorts in these scenic hills, the pleasure of a stay in a tea estate is unsurpassed, especially for the tea lover.

Nonsuch Tea Estate offers Nonsuch Retreat, a charming bungalow surrounded by English country lawns at a vantage height, from where one enjoys the twinkling lights of the plains of the town on the northern side and the plains of Karamadai on its southern overlook.

As a passing visitor, it is well its worth to visit the well-known Highlands Tea Estate, that has tours of its gardens and factory. Equally historic, Glendale Tea Estates Ltd and Waterfalls Estates Pvt. Ltd have guest houses at Glendale, Adderley and Runnymede in Coonoor, and the Waterfall Ropeway Bungalow in Valparai. Their gardens were set up by the Stanes family whose ancestors ventured into the Nilgiris in 1852 to set up coffee plantations.

Guests can enjoy witnessing the production of their quality teas, including limited amounts of handmade tea. Similarly, the Woodbriars Group offer stays at 'Briar Tea Bungalows' at their gardens in Valparai, Munnar and Meghamalai.

Set in a dreamy location amidst soft clouds that flit in and out of the tea bushes, one might even chance a glimpse of elephants strolling through the gardens, some of them being located close-by in wildlife sanctuaries.

A Taste of South India

South India is the primeval land of the Dravidians, with a chequered history of kingdoms and great rulers, of invasions and colonisation. It held a position of significance in ancient times, its southern coastline afforded a trading link between the Mediterranean and the Far East.

The Greeks, Romans, Arabs, Jews and Chinese all came here, lured by indigo, spices and silks, that comprised the Indian treasury for barter.

This region also saw great rivalry among the Portuguese, French and the British, as they established individual pockets of sway. One such enclave was Fort St George on the Coromandel Coast that had been purchased

RIGHT: The organic Korakundah Tea Estate of the United Nilgiris Tea Estate Co Ltd is at the highest altitude in South India.

from the local ruler by Francis Day of the East India Company in 1639. Later, it fell into French hands, but after bitter warfare, the British managed to wrest it back and consolidate more areas around it, so that by 1774, the Madras Presidency had been created. This then, was the birth of present-day Chennai. South India was reorganised after independence along linguistic lines into the states of Andhra Pradesh, Karnataka, Kerala and Tamil Nadu.

Together, these make up peninsular India, a huge inverted triangle that juts out into the Indian Ocean, bound by the Bay of Bengal in the east and the Arabian Sea on the west. While it encloses the Deccan Plateau in its womb, its coastline is bordered by hilly ghats.

Known as the Sahyadris, the Western Ghats, are steeper than the Eastern Ghats, and they run all the way south. As an extension, the Nilgiris form a crescent along the borders of the states of Tamil Nadu, northern Kerala and Karnataka.

The Palakkad and Wayanad hills, the Satyamangalam hills, as well as the Tirupati and Anamalai hills are also encompassed within these ranges. It was in these tropical elevations that, under the British colonisers, experiments with growing tea proved successful.

Tea regions in the south have interesting regional facets of their own. The people and their towns reveal varied lifestyles. Village homes and carved temple gopurams in Tamil Nadu dot the lush valleys with their vibrant colours whereas gleaming whitewashed houses with clay tiled roofs and spired churches and minarets of mosques peep through thick coconut groves across Kerala's countryside as Christians and Muslims were brought in by missionaries and traders that came from the sea routes into ancient Kerala ports.

The south, therefore, is a potpourri of cultures, symbolised as it were, by the many distinctions of its tea characters.

Ootacamund

The course of history took a turn when, in the eighteenth century, the great Muslim king, Tipu Sultan of Mysore, surrendered this region to the conquering British.

The new rulers liked this scenic land, bought up vast tracts from the local Toda and Irumba tribes at a pittance, often just the price of a few meals. Consequently by mid-nineteenth century, the hill town of Ootacamund, or Udhagamandalam as it was known in its earliest days, was seeing development and today, it is the headquarters of the Nilgiri district.

Popularly referred to as Ooty, the town is best approached by a road journey from the town of Coimbatore, in the foothills, that has a tea auction centre. The climb is steep and rapid, through wooded hairpin bends.

A more leisurely alternative may be to take the metre gauge 'toy train' of the Nilgiri Mountain Railway (NMR) that starts from Mettupalayam. This Swiss-engineered train, another late nineteenth-century remnant of the Raj, is considered an extension to the World Heritage Site of the Darjeeling Himalayan Railway by the UNESCO.

Ooty town, although getting overwhelmed by urbanisation, is embossed with history. John Sullivan's

'Stone House' is now a part of the Government Arts College. The Gothic-style nineteenth century St Stephen's Church has huge wooden beams that were hauled by elephants from Tipu Sultan's palace in Srirangapatnam. Another heritage spot is the botanical gardens built around an artificial lake, constructed in the year 1824.

There are some colonial hotels like The Taj Savoy of the Tata Group's Indian Hotels Company Limited. Its English-style cottages date back to 1835, with ancient

FACING PAGE: The woven wrap and hair in ringlets is an attire that is curious only to Toda tribal women.

ABOVE: This quaint Toda hutment is rather uncommon to come by nowadays. Toda lands are considered a part of the UNESCO-designated International Biosphere Reserve.

fireplaces that still work. Similarly, ITC WelcomHeritage Fernhills Royale Palace has the distinction of being the first English property to be bought by a wealthy Indian royal of the Wodeyar line of princes in 1873.

The Ootacamund Club with its period décor is perhaps the best preserved of old English clubs in the country. The Club started as lavishly designed hotel owned by a wealthy Englishman. It became a club in 1841 for the military elite; tea planters were also invited to its membership. Sporting traditions like golf at Wenlock Downs, or the Ootacmund Derby, a high season event, live on.

This region's tea history can be gathered at the Dodabetta Tea Museum where the visitor is greeted by the pungent-sweet aroma of tea being manufactured at its tea factory.

Coonoor

Coonoor, besides its charming hilly setting of tea gardens, also has the distinction of housing the eminent

Defence Services Staff College besides its superbly ordered military cantonment, named after Sir Arthur Wellesley, the Duke of Wellington. Its impressive barracks were completed in 1860, and there is a museum that chronicles the bravery of the Madras Regiment that is headquartered here. The regiment was instituted by Colonel Robert Clive who laid siege to the French at Fort St George in 1758 and wrested it from them, laying down the origins of Chennai.

It was, perhaps but a natural choice for the heroic Late Field Marshall Sam Maneckshaw to make his home in these evocative surroundings. He would have, in all probability, enjoyed a round of golf at the notable Wellington Club, or savoured his cup of tea while appreciating the enchanting views of the seemingly endless tea estates from his balcony.

Idukki District

It is in the ancient trading centre of Cochin, now called Kochi, that the Portuguese first gained a concession from

FACING PAGE: The Nilgiri Mountain Railway steams into Lovedale, a stop just before Ooty.

ABOVE: The historic Madras Regimental Centre.

BELOW: The museum exhibits the early infantry of the Regiment, being the very first brigade to be raised by the East India Company.

OVERLEAF: A typically overcast evening sky over a tea estate in the Nilgiris ranges.

the original rulers of the Varma dynasty. Then came the Dutch, from whom the British negotiated to gain a small enclave in Willingdon Island.

Here too, came the Jews who sought refuge as they fled during the Crusades in the medieval period. Their history lives on in Jew Town, Mattancherry. Even today, the old town of Fort Kochi remains in a time warp, with its cobbled streets, quaint cafés and heritage buildings.

Among the most remarkable attractions here are the Chinese fishing nets that loom in the horizon of Kochi beach. They are contrived by a rather unique system of cantilevered fixed land installations that lower the gigantic nets into the sea for bringing in the catch, and are said to have been discovered by Zheng He, a Chinese explorer.

In this land of palm-fringed waterways fed by rivers and the backwaters of the sea, the ghats afford pleasing drives that wind through coffee and rubber plantations. Many of the tea gardens lie adjacent to tracts of cardamom plantings and spice gardens of cloves, turmeric and cashew.

In other places, the plantations may have musky peppercorn or fragrant vanilla vines twining around the shade trees, for this is the famed 'land of spice'. Its lush tropical ecosphere also creates wildlife sanctuaries like Thekkady and Periyar, through which the road passes on the way to Munnar.

Munnar

Endowed with a location that has given it a name that translates as 'three rivers', Munnar is a town so essentially scenic that it attracts tourists aplenty.

Besides several hotels suited for all budgets, it has a buzzing downtown bazaar with shops that sell tea spices and herbal oils, that are a bounty of this region. The surrounding countryside is a little piece of paradise. Silvery waterfalls fuelled by frequent rain showers echo melodiously through the velvet green faces of the mountains.

Once in twelve years, these hills undergo a divine transformation, when they get carpeted by Neelakurinchi

or Strobilanthus, a species of wild orchids that cast a violet glow over the entire landscape.

The magic of nature continues with scenic places like Anayirankal Dam and Pothamedu, Sita Devi Lake near the small hill station of Devikulam, Mattupetty Lake, cascading waterfalls at Attukal and Nyayamakad and romantic misty views at Lock Heart Gap with its Echo Point. Maravoor, a short distance further, is famed for its fragrant sandalwood trees. The thick tropical forests on the hills give rise to wildlife viewing.

The Eravikulam National Park in the vicinity, is home to the Nilgiri Tahr, a rare mountain goat that is distinctive only to these parts. Closer to the Tamil Nadu border, lies the Chinnar Wildlife Sanctuary. These are some of the many charms that enhance the pleasure of visiting Munnar's beautiful tea gardens.

Throughout this unsullied region, jungles continue their spread. The Tirunelveli district, further south, has a bucolic beauty with small settlements around the tea plantations and soothing viewpoints like Kuthiravetti and the scenic Upper Kodaiyar Dam.

Amongst these highlights, it is worthwhile to visit nearby Kanyakumari, the last land stop at the tip of India. Beyond, lies the overwhelming vastness of the Indian Ocean, reaching out to neighbouring Sri Lanka, where the British planted tea after their success in India.

Hassan

Hassan, in Karnataka, is the cradle of the ancient Dravidian kingdom. Its Hindu antecedents are expressed in intricately carved temples, as in the twelfth century Chennakaseva temple complex in Belur which was the early capital of the Hoysala Empire. Halebid is another temple town close by.

FACING PAGE Chinese fishing nets, so named as they are believed to have been introduced by a Chinese explorer, are a landmark at the Fort Kochi beach.
ABOVE: Anayirankal Dam just outside Munnar is surrounded by tea gardens.
OVERLEAF: A panorama of rolling hills sheathed in tea bushes unfolds around Munnar.

Coorg

On the same circuit, there is Coorg or Kodagu with its
ethnic Kodava community, an ancient martial race with
a distinct culture. It is known for the physically beautiful
attributes of its people and environs. Its cool, hilly
terrain, thick forests, orange orchards, paddy fields,
and a large spread of coffee plantations include some tea
gardens as well.

In all, the Nilgiri mountain ranges with their humid, cool
clime together with the coastal ghats combine to define the
exceptional geography of these southern states soaked in
history and endowed with nature's bounty. It is, perhaps,
this unmatched splendour that contributes to the unique
aroma and richness of the tea from this region.

ABOVE: The twelfth century Chennakesava Temple of the Hoysala
kings at Belur.
FACING PAGE: Peppercorn vines twine around shade trees in a
Kerala tea plantation, while cardamom plantings prosper at its edges.

BOUQUET OF REGIONAL TEAS

'Its liquor is like the sweetest dew from Heaven.'

~ *Lu Yu*

Apart from its three main regional tea-growing belts, India has a posy of smaller tea growing pockets that make a discrete, though important, contribution to the country's total output of the produce.

Moreover, effectively these are 'practical' teas, as they are relatively inexpensive. Being more affordable, they find a ready home in the country's enormous domestic market, besides being preferred by buyers for making blends.

These pockets are located along the foothills of the Himalayas that crowns the country, and comprise regions in the North-east, the North as well as the North-west. Apart from the well-known foothill regions of Dooars and Terai, there are six states other than Assam that make up the North-east and these also contribute to tea production, the major share coming from Tripura.

In the North and the North-western Himalayan regions, tea estates in the valleys of Uttarakhand close to the state capital of Dehradun, produce organic teas, some of which are remarkable for their quality and flavour. Kangra Valley in the North-West chiefly produces green tea, but its Orthodox black tea is also known for its delicate character. These teas are valued highly in the international markets for their quality and flavour. Kangra tea has been accorded GI certificate at the national level.

FACING PAGE: [TOP] Hoodle Tea Estate of Dharamshala Tea Company produces quality Orthodox teas.
[BELOW] Kangra Valley tea gardens sometimes employ both male and female pluckers to surmount labour problems.

Teas from Dooars & Terai

Lying in the plains of Darjeeling around Jalpaiguri and Cooch Behar and in some parts of Assam, the Dooars region has an abundant yield of tea. Its low fertile hills, ranging from altitudes of 90 to 1750 metres above sea level, are fed by innumerable streams and rivers that are fuelled by heavy rains.

Extreme humidity results in a faster growth of the tea bushes. As a result, although this region does not have many tea estates—approximately 3,150** gardens in all, it produces a fair quantity, approximately 147.59 million kg* of tea, annually, a figure which indicates that the produce per unit is high. Many large tea companies like McLeod Russel, Goodricke, Duncan Industries, Octavius Tea & Industries, have their plantations here in addition to a host of local growers.

Dooars teas are somewhat like those of Assam and are largely CTC, with a strong and full-bodied character. Although they tend to be grainy, these teas have great value as their strong colour makes them an ideal component for blending. On its own, Dooars tea can be a good daytime tea, taken with milk. Another tea belt of notable worth is the marshy Terai that lies in the southern foothills of the Himalayas that also covers parts of Nepal. With a similar climate of moisture-filled low elevations, it has many more tea gardens than the Dooars, 7,062** in number. However, its produce is lesser, about 112.82 million kg* of tea. The quality of leaf emits a richly coloured brew with a spicy taste.

Tea from Extreme North-East

Tea cultivation is also being promoted beyond the Assam corridor to the 'sister' states that extend further into the north-eastern confines of the country, bordering neighbouring Bangladesh. Here, in this similar topography of low elevations and humidity, the State of Tripura has the largest yield, producing almost 7.8 million kg** of tea every year. Combined with the states of Arunachal Pradesh, Manipur, Nagaland, Meghalaya, Sikkim and Mizoram this region makes up a worthy output of approximately 15 million kg** of tea, which is mostly CTC.

North-Western Himalayan Tea

Being conversant with the climatic and topographical requisites for tea cultivation, British tea planters began to make the most of the geographical assets of the land. They moved westwards, along the Himalayan ranges that unfold over the northern boundaries of India, to create a sprinkling of tea-growing pockets.

Amongst these, small scale tea gardens were developed around Vikasnagar, near Dehradun, the present capital of the State of Uttarakhand. With gardens that nestle in low elevations of 452 metres, these heritage gardens produce some high quality tea for export.

Not far from here, a two-hour road journey away, it is worthwhile to make a diversion to visit the picturesque pilgrimage town of Haridwar. Located on the banks of the River Ganges, the waters of which are considered the holiest in India, it is dotted with innumerable temples and yogic ashrams that lend spiritual respite to hundreds of seekers.

In the evening, fervent devotees dedicate oil lamps in flower-filled floating baskets to the river. East of Haridwar and up in the Kumaon Hills, the state has developed some more small scale tea gardens in the Kasauni and Almora districts that are of high standards. Being relatively young, the teas they produce are very flavoury, and these are being successfully exported.

LEFT: Tea bushes in the Valley thrive in the shadow of the misty Dhauladhars. The tea gardens suffered a setback after the great earthquake of 1905.

Green & Black Kangra Valley Teas

Of all the north Himalayan posse of teas, the district of Kangra Valley in the State of Himachal Pradesh that borders Punjab reigns supreme. Although this region is small, its produce nevertheless carries a name in world markets. Tea arrived in Kangra Valley almost at the same time as it did in Darjeeling. Initially, black tea manufacture was considered the domain of the settlers, and green tea was made by the native proprietors as its manufacture required very little machinery.

Even to this day, this region continues to be associated with green tea although eighty-five per cent of the produce is black tea. However, the total production in numbers is not large, approximately 850,000 kg of tea*. Moreover this area, which includes parts of Chamba

and Mandi districts of Himachal Pradesh, consists mostly of gardens that are more in the nature of small holdings, having been fragmented over the years in the process of being passed down as family inheritances. The industry being on such a small scale, the leaf is grown entirely in the organic way, and the manufacture is wholly Orthodox.

As the tea originates from the China seed, its black tea flavours retain a unique character, derived from its old, slow growing bushes: so that Kangra tea has been

ABOVE: A young girl in a Kangra Valley tea garden is intent on plucking the leaf. Her dress expresses the proximity of Kangra to Punjab.

ABOVE: A tea garden in Tripura.

BELOW: Like most of the tea gardens in Uttarakhand, Ghorakhal Tea Estate grows tea the organic way.

accorded the GI certification on the national level. In fact, there is great optimism that it can qualify to be ranked with Darjeeling tea in the international arena in the future.

The flavours of Kangra tea, no doubt, are comparable to those of the Darjeeling leaf, although they do not have the same astringency. Being mellow and smooth with a lower caffeine content, they can be consumed several times through the day. Their sweetish undertones can be well enjoyed without milk or sugar.

In particular, First Flush tea, with their delicate aromas and hints of fruity flavours are very well-rated and fetch high prices in the market.

In general, Kangra teas have a light gold colour with a clear liquor, making them well suited for ready-to-drink teas as well as iced tea.

Under the British, the area flourished primarily as a tea-growing district and the town of Palampur did so well that the British seriously considered making it the summer capital. The Gazetteer of The Kangra district (1882–83), Volume 1 recorded that: 'The tea now made is probably superior to that produced anywhere else in India. The demand has been steadily increasing and much is now bought by natives for export via Peshawar to Kabul and Central Asia.' Kangra tea also reached European markets through the UK, Spain and Holland and even won gold and silver medals at exhibitions in European capitals during 1886–95.

Unfortunately, by a sad quirk of fate, in 1905, the fortunes of Kangra Valley changed when it was devastated by a great earthquake. The tea factories lay in ruins and the panic-stricken planters began to make distress sales, hurriedly handing over the estates to either their workers or local traders.

As the facilities for black tea production were disrupted, green tea manufacture became the norm and over the years it has developed a market that is especially appreciated in Kashmir, Afghanistan, Central Asia and the Middle East.

However, Kangra Valley, in a sense, still remains bruised by its setbacks. There are acute labour problems and as a result, tea cultivation here has come to be more in the nature of a cottage industry, with many growers resorting to growing cash crops as supplementary income. The small garden owners send their leaf to

FACING PAGE: A weathered face with a kindly smile. An ethnic inhabitant of Kangra Valley.

ABOVE: Tea pluckers in Kangra return after a workday. The leaf is sent to factory co-operatives.

OVERLEAF: Close-up of the tea bushes.

factory cooperatives. Some large growers, however, do produce well-known brands like 'Wah Tea', 'Him Tea', 'Manjhee Valley Tea', and 'Himalayan Kangra Tea'.

Among the largest is G.M.S. Mann's Dharamsala Tea Company that produces white, black, oolong and green teas in its own garden tea factory, where visitors are welcome. It is located in the upper reaches of the mountains, in Narghota village, closer to the quaint town of Dharamsala.

ABOVE: Palampur is set in the midst of the tea gardens, where one can walk through narrow paths among the bushes.

The Romance of Tea Estates

Palampur, the main tea growing area, derives its name from the word *pulum* meaning 'lots of water'. It is laced by several rivulets and streams, while in some places the roar of the Bundla River chasm breaks the silence of the quiet estates.

Unlike Darjeeling or Ooty, where one has to make an excursion to visit tea plantations, the town is actually set upon the tea gardens, so that one can amble through the narrow paths between the bushes. Smiling Gorkha tea pickers, their cheeks made radiant by the pristine

ABOVE: [CLOCKWISE FROM TOP]

Not far from the tea gardens His Holiness, the Dalai Lama, has set up his seat-in-exile at Mcleodganj;

Trinkets like friendship bands, add colour to the crowded bazaars of Mcleodganj;

Norbulingka Institute near Dharamshala encourages the preservation of Tibetan culture.

environment, dot the gardens. As in Darjeeling, their ancestors migrated from Nepal to provide a labour bank for the British planters.

A visitor can opt for a stay in Himachal State Tourism's Hotel T-Bud that is located in the midst of a tea garden.

It is also possible to enjoy a homestay in time honoured family-run tea gardens such as Darang Tea Estate. This has the distinction of being owned by the first woman planter in this area, Sarla Bhandari, and is currently run by the fifth generation. Here it is possible to enjoy a cup of tea in its charmingly English veranda with wicker chairs and potted plants.

Some royal properties, like ITC WelcomHeritage's Taragarh Palace Hotel offer a peek into the past. Built by the Nawab of Bhawalpur as a summer resort, Taragarh Palace was later bought by the royal family of Jammu and Kashmir.

The past resonates in the lounge of this resort with its classic draped doors and walls adorned with tiger skins, together with an ornate mirror and old photographs.

It was built in the 1930s and has European-style architecture, as several of the princes, including the Nawab of Bhawalpur whose palace it was, were exposed to lavish western tastes.

PREVIOUS PAGE: Sounds of temple bells and conch shells, a glow of oil lamps, the fragrance of incense—these are some of the sights, sounds and smells that one comes across as dusk gathers over the pilgrimage town of Haridwar that lies on the banks of the holy river, Ganges. During festival time, hordes of devotees throng its banks to offer prayers. A short distance away, in the low hills around the neighbouring city of Dehradun in Uttarakhand, there are some tea gardens which produce small quantities of quality tea that is exported.

RIGHT: The past resonates in the lounge of ITC WelcomHeritage's Taragarh Palace.

A Taste of Kangra Valley

Kangra Valley was the battleground for several invaders who came through its north-western Himalayan passes. It was here that the Greek king Alexander the Great, (c. 320 BC) fought the local king Poros, who is identified by historians as Paramanand Chandra, of the Katoch family lineage. In the year AD 1009, the Muslim warrior, Mahmud of Ghazni, laid siege to the town of Kangra. He is said to have plundered a huge booty from eight secret wells inside its fort.

> One of the earliest are its unique nomadic pastoral tribes, known as the Gaddis. It is believed that they fled here from the plains during the seventeenth century to take shelter from persecution by the Mughal emperor, Aurangzeb. The tribes have a remarkable knowledge of the countryside, including the ability to forecast the weather with great accuracy.

A distinct Hindu culture is manifested in the several ancient temples that dot the countryside. Temples like Brijeshwar, Chamunda Mandir, Ashapurni Mandir and several others abound with mythological lore. One of the best-known of these, Baijnath Temple, is dedicated to Lord Shiva, 'Lord of the Mountains', who is also called Vaidyanath, 'Lord of Physicians'.

Not far from Palampur, some thirty-eight kilometres away, the Dhauladhar heights tower above Kangra Valley, and reverberate with Buddhist chants. It is to these hills that the great leader of Tibetan Buddhism, His Holiness, The Dalai Lama, migrated in 1959 to set up his government-in-exile at Mcleodganj, in the suburbs of Dharamsala. Devotees the world over, including well-known Hollywood stars, throng here to pay homage to their spiritual leader. The town is like a little piece of Tibet, with its characteristic monasteries and narrow bazaars selling votive objects, beaded jewellery and handicrafts, carpets, *thangka* paintings and fascinating knick knacks. Its several cafes and bakeries emit aromas of European food, which caters to tourists, as well as local thupka or Tibetan fare. Once again, glimpses of colonial history are revealed at St. John's Church in the Wilderness that has a monument dedicated to Lord Elgin, one of the viceroys of India, who died while touring here. Around 1848, the British had annexed this area, and set up a cantonment at Yol for their Gorkha troops who served them during the First World War.

It is not surprising that this quaint region has been an inspiration for some of the country's finest art, giving rise to the historical Kangra school of miniature paintings. It is said that the invasion of Delhi by Nadir Shah in 1739 caused several artists to flee here.

They continued to paint, mixing the delicate Mughal style with Hindu themes. The Sobha Singh painting gallery, as well as the artist's village at Andretta, near Palampur, are a treat for the art lover. Besides being home to tea, the Kangra region has preserved its past

within the folds of its magnificent Dhauladhar ranges. Be it the omnipresent tea stall outside the local Hindu temple, or the Buddhist monk sipping a steaming mug of tea—the mysticism and culture of this land is evident everywhere for all to see.

FACING PAGE: Visitors spin prayer wheels going around the spectacular stupa of the Namgyal Monastery.

ABOVE: [CLOCKWISE FROM LEFT] A young and pensive 'little Buddha'; The imposing altar of the Buddha; Finishing touches to a *thangka* painting; Monks at Dip-Tse-Chok-Ling Monastery in Mcleodganj.

Tea Board Logos for Indian Teas

Darjeeling Tea

Darjeeling tea, with its own special character, is manifested as such in the Tea Board's logo. It depicts the figure of a woman tea-picker holding the tea leaf tenderly. No doubt, it is a boon of Nature expressed by the colour green that represents the fragrance of Darjeeling tea, so delicate and aromatic.

Assam Tea

The Tea Board of India has epitomised the character of Assam tea appropriately in its logo. It depicts the tea leaf above the one-horned rhinoceros, a species typical to these parts and considered the official state animal. The full-bodied strength and jungle origins of this tea are expressed by this animal, matchless in strength and size, even while subsisting on a purely herbivorous diet. The reddish-brown imprint represents the colour of the brew, Orthodox Assam Teas producing a lighter shade than those produced by the CTC method of production.

Kangra Tea

Kangra tea owes much to the spectacular Dhauladhar ranges that preside over its Valley, as moisture-filled clouds collide against their mighty heights and foster the tea bushes with frequent showers of rain. The Tea Board logo pays tribute to these ranges by showcasing them in their logo, crowned by the omnipresent tea leaf.

Dooars & Terai

Both these regions have commanded a significant position as a part of the treasury of Indian teas from the early days, when the industry first took birth in this country. The Tea Board of India has therefore deemed it fit to bestow them with a common logo as they have a similarity of backdrop and character. The elephant, native to the jungles that dominate the countryside, announces the vigour of the brew that is derived from the tea leaf that is typical to these parts.

Nilgiri Tea

Both Nilgiri Orthodox and CTC tea has been accredited with its own logo by the Tea Board. In a shade of purple-blue, it shows the tea leaf against the backdrop of mountain silhouettes that represent the Nilgiris or 'Blue Mountains'. No doubt this flavourful and prolific yield owes much to these humid, cool mountain ranges as well as the coastal ghats that constitute the exceptional geography of this land.

Logos of a few private tea companies and estates

FROM THE LEAF TO THE **SIP**

It is 8:00 a.m. in Assam, and in the sprawling tea gardens of Assam Company Limited's Greenwood Tea Estate, plucking activity is making a start. In the rest of the country, the time is 7:00 a.m., but here in this extreme north-eastern part of the country, the sun makes an early appearance. As though to 'catch' the day, several tea estates move forward their clocks to follow their own garden or *bagan* time, a tradition that carries on from the British times.

FACING PAGE: [CLOCKWISE FROM TOP LEFT]

Bird's eye view of tea terraces;

A plucker hard at work;

Fibre extractor removing woody fluff from leaves;

Transporting leaf to the co-operatives factory.

ABOVE: The tea leaf that endows the brew.
FACING PAGE: A worker in a tea garden in Kangra Valley deftly snaps
the two-leaves-and-a-bud.

PLUCKING THE LEAF

'So I must rise at early dawn, as busy as can be, to get my daily labour done and pick the leafy tea.'

~ *Lu Yu*

The tranquil and rather somnolent vistas of a tea plantation belie the toil and industrious activity involved in nurturing the tea bushes to yield the brew. The tea plant is unique, and has a sensitive temperament, so its leaf must be harvested with a specialised skill. The quality of the end product will depend largely on the selective plucking of the tea leaves, a delicate task, best performed by a woman's hand.

Considering that tea gardens run into thousands of hectares, there is a huge labour force at work, predominantly female. Most of them work and live in special housing 'lines' within the gardens. This is a system that evolved under the British pioneers, who brought in workers from outlying regions as the plantations began to flourish.

Over the ages, generations of families have continued to work and live in these plantations. They look to the manager as the *burra sahib*, the 'big boss', just as they did to the colonial planters of yesteryears.

The British era of tea in India has long gone. However, set as they are, in a remote and isolated milieu, life on these tea plantations has not much changed.

Tea cultivation, no doubt, has made several advances under scientific and improved agro-practices. Some mechanisation has also been introduced to pluck the leaf.

Still, human toil cannot be replaced entirely, even as the bushes continue to flourish as mute witnesses to the passages of time.

Life of a Tea Plant

The dew has still not dried on the bush and the leaves exude a delicate fragrance. The cold winter is practically over, so that the bushes are now emerging from dormancy, or the *banjhi* phase, to give forth the first flush. The young terminal *banjhi* bud has unfurled and cast off both its scales or *janams* as the locals call it, to reveal the characteristic scar marks on the stem.

Between the *janam* and leaf, is another appendage, the fish leaf. With the swelling of the bud, *janams*, fish leaf and normal leaves will be produced in quick succession. All these appendages with their axil buds will start producing normal shoots of considerable vigour, ready to be plucked.

After this first flush, the shoot will go into brief dormancy and take almost two weeks or more to emerge once again for the next flush, depending on the plucking system and climatic conditions. For instance, during the rainy period or the monsoon flush, the shoots will emerge much faster due to the increased humidity, while the autumn flush yield will not be so prolific.

Come winter and the bushes go into a long dormancy, so that it is time to attend to activities that will lay the ground for a good output during the next season. This is also pruning time and sections of the tea estates reveal the dwarfed brown forms of the bushes, their stunted bare branches waiting to get clothed again with healthy new leaf for plucking. Some tracts are hard pruned, while others may have lightly pruned or 'skiffed' bushes, as staggered pruning will ensure that there is a continuous yield of leaf buds during the flushes.

The Assam bush spreads out from a single tree-like trunk, whereas bushes that thrive from the parent stock of Chinese seedlings have a multi-stem character. In either case, the pretty buttercup-shaped pale creamy yellow flower which is a natural bloom of the Camellia Sinensis or the tea plant is not utilised; it sacrifices its beauty for the sake of the leaf and is rarely seen as the bushes are kept pruned to a height of about 90 cm–120 cm for ease of plucking and a healthy yield. The value, rather, is placed only on the terminal buds with two or more young leaves that will be plucked, depending on the end quality of tea to be produced in the factory.

LEFT: This pretty buttercup shaped flower of the Camellia Sinensis, the tea plant, is rare to see, as the bushes are kept consistently pruned to stimulate vigorous new shoots.

A good quality Assam tea plant may have a productive life of fifty years and more, but a China hybrid grown in the higher elevations of Darjeeling is more resilient and can flourish up to seventy or eighty years. Some of the original tea bushes from the China seeds may even be 150 years old. Companies ensure that at any given time, the next generation of tea bushes is under preparation. The McLeod Russel tea gardens dedicate two per cent of their land acreage to replanting annually so that every fifty years there will be a new bush that will start to produce leaves for the first picking after about four years from planting. Similarly, Apeejay Tea has been carrying out a rejuvenation program over the last decade under which roughly fourteen per cent of their land area of 50,000 acres has been replanted with young teas. In this manner, the ecological balance of the tea gardens is always kept maintained.

that nourish the fallow land for two years. It is only then that seedlings from the carefully tended nurseries are laid out; a quick method of propagation is through clonal planting.

Several plantations therefore prefer to employ a mix of Assam hybrid and China hybrid cloned varieties besides developing new plantings from seeds. Gardens have a programme to plant young tea bushes annually so that there will be a next generation of bushes that will be ready for plucking every fourth year. Plantations therefore usually combine seed planting with propagation through clonal planting that is much quicker, although in the latter case, a disease attack can affect the entire crop. Large tea companies conduct a continuous, well calculated activity to ensure that the next generation of tea bushes will always be ready to maintain the ecology of their tea gardens.

A lengthy process of preparation is involved to cultivate the new tea bushes. Guatemala grasses are first grown

ABOVE: Plucking the leaf under hothouse weather conditions in Assam is no easy task.

ABOVE: [CLOCKWISE FROM TOP]

Workers busy plucking in a tea estate in Darjeeling;

The Assam tea bush has a single tree-like trunk and large, hardy leaves;

These tea seeds will involve a lengthy time span before they take on the form of new tea bushes.

OVERLEAF: A tea nursery at McLeod Russel's Sepon Tea Estate in Assam.

Plucking the Leaf 157

In his book on Williamson Magor, *Four Mangoe Lane: The First Address in Tea*, Sujoy Gupta quotes from an internal note written by a partner in 1949 that describes the firm's views on nurturing of the tea plant.

> 'With tea it is continuity of method that counts so much, and in the years which follow one another throughout the life of this plant, it is knowing what to do at every stage that really matters. After all, your capital is your tea bush…' (Gupta: 2001).

Agro activity on a tea estate is a complex affair, with constant research and technological advances taking place continuously and constantly.

A Workday in the Tea Gardens

It is the beginning of March and the end of winter, when a light morning mist still hangs over the tea bushes. In Darjeeling, where the Himalayas take longer to cast off their winter mantle, first flush pickings will commence three weeks later, towards end March and early April; in the south, however, as the seasons do not change their moods, the plucking of the leaf carries on throughout the year.

Be it anywhere, the morning activity in a tea garden is the same: a ripple of voices and a jingle of bangles fill the air as rows of women queue up for attendance in the factory outhouse to set off towards their assigned

tea leaf plucking areas. A large tea estate has hundreds of workers and they are allocated into groups, each assigned different tasks. Their areas are divided into divisions and sections very much in the manner of a military platoon, being administered by a hierarchical reporting system consisting of assistant managers, section managers and foremen.

They maintain a detailed record of the harvesting and plucking rounds in the sections and also keep track of the picking cycles, as during the flushing period, the leaf is ready to be plucked every 5–10 days in each area.

The women weave through the rows of tea bushes in traditional colourful clothing, cloth hampers or wicker baskets on their back, held in place by a band slung over a small padding on their covered head.

Using both hands, with practised agility, they deftly snap the 'two leaves and a bud' for a fine plucking that goes to make superlative teas; for the more common teas, they might pluck three, four or five leaves, depending on the directive of the estate manager. To relieve their tedium, the women sometimes break into song. At other times they might pause to refresh themselves with salted tea which they carry in a flask slung across their waist. They work indefatigably, even during the rains, when they continue plucking, wearing gumboots, supporting umbrellas or donning raincoats.

The men do the heavy work like pruning, digging drains and clearing the undergrowth to prepare the land for planting.

During the course of the day, workers make two or three trips to unload their harvest at the weighing station in their section, where their effort is registered. A picker would have harvested almost 2,000–4,000 stems for a single kilogram of green leaf which, after being processed in the factory, would yield approximately 215 grams of made tea, depending on the leaf variety.

FACING PAGE: Women pluckers bring in the leaf at the end of a day in a tea garden in upper Assam. Male workers are employed to do the heavy tasks.

ABOVE: Sacks of freshly plucked tea leaves are loaded on a three-tiered trailer to keep the leaf from different plucking sections segregated.

This clearly indicates the diligence and tedium of their daily toil. They would need to pluck approximately sixty green shoots (that comprise 15 gms of green leaf) to make up a teaspoon measure (2–3 gms) of the processed leaf used to prepare a single cup of the brew.

Large tea estates usually have the tea factory on the premises. As the leaves get heated up rapidly and begin changing chemically if left in the basket for even an hour, they must be taken quickly for processing. As a result, factories work unceasingly through the night, while those in the garden return home to sleep to start another day early next morning.

FACING PAGE: Workers make periodic rounds at the weighing stations that are situated in each section of the garden, to have their toil weighed and recorded.

ABOVE: Workers make their way to a tea factory at the end of the day.

OVERLEAF: A woman prepares tea for the male hands before they set out for their morning shift at the tea factory.

A Worker's Life

Aruna must rise in the shadowy light of the dawn. Somewhere a rooster calls and the goats in the compound bleat in unison.

It is time to do the morning chores for the household and ready her children for school before she leaves her bamboo-fenced homestead and dons her wicker basket to report for her plucking assignment. Her husband drives a tea trailer in the garden. When she returns at sundown, she will busy herself with cooking the evening meal. Her children would already be home, but she has nothing to worry, as their school is nearby in the compound itself, and they have a playground to keep them happy.

Plantation worker's lives are more or less similar anywhere in India. Most of them live in the residential 'lines' that are provided within the estates. The Plantation Labour Act makes it mandatory for the management to look after the all-inclusive needs of its workers.

A large tea estate must have a hospital, a school, a water reservoir and even places of worship, besides providing social welfare benefits like subsidised rations, mosquito nets and firewood.

On weekends and holidays, the workers go to local markets or *haats*, celebrating festivals with cockfights and colourful dances. In this sequestered world of the tea plantations, several generations of worker families have been living on the estates for more than a century, having known no other way of life.

Many of their predecessors, however, witnessed tortuous times under the early planters. By the 1860s, as the tea industry prospered, local workforce was not enough and the British began to hire contractors and agents to import labourers from tribal areas from the then Central Provinces, Bihar and Orissa (now Odisha), besides southern Nepal. These middlemen would lure poor peasants and pack them into overcrowded boats in merciless conditions. Several died of starvation and disease like typhoid, diarrhoea and malaria during the long and tortuous journey up the river to Assam.

A document submitted by A. Mackenzie, official Secretary to the Government of Bengal in 1873 reported:

'It seems that in the first three years after Act III of 1863 which allowed the services of contractors came into operation, the deaths in the contractors' depots and on the voyage up amounted to more than 5,000 out of a total of over 90,000 labourers recruited.' (Bengal Secretariat Press: 1873).

On reaching the plantations, their sad plight continued, in fact worsened, as they were segregated in 'coolie lines' or quarters on the estates in conditions similar to concentration camps, and were subjected to tough military discipline. Mackenzie goes on to report:

'It is not surprising that during these evil times, the idea of escaping was always present to [in] the coolies' minds and it was equally natural that planters should do all in their power to prevent it. Chowkidars were posted at every possible outlet from the coolie lines which in some cases were enclosed by high palisades, outside which the coolies were not allowed at night.'

In Darjeeling, the labour situation was better. Dr Campbell requested a visiting Nepalese nobleman Sri Dakman Rai, to send labourers from Nepal for which he gave grants of freehold lands in return so that families settle down in the gardens. However, even in the south, poor peasants were brought in, mostly from Salem district, and made to work in dire conditions.

By 1882, the Bengali intelligentsia started a movement to protect the labourers and by the turn of the century, the outlook had improved.

Planters began to realise the value of labour and started giving out pieces of government *khas* or special land to those whose contracts had expired so that they could do their own farming and maintain poultry and livestock. In this way, the settled population grew and it provided a bank of casual labour during the plucking season.

In other cases, the planter had to house the labour, and take care of all their personal living needs besides paying higher wages. As a result, while local towns developed

outside, more and more workers chose to stay on in the gardens and adopt the way of life there.

Roopali, who works as a housemaid in an upscale residence in Delhi, has a lot to say. Her high-boned cheeks reflect the features of a hill woman as she speaks with a faraway look about her childhood in the mountains of Jalpaiguri near Darjeeling where her father has just

FACING PAGE: Setting out for the tea gardens.
ABOVE: [CLOCKWISE FROM TOP]
A mud-plastered-bamboo dwelling of a tea worker in Assam;
Tea countryside is dotted with little townships as workers whose contracts in the gardens had expired under the planters, chose to settle down outside;
Aruna, a plucker on Darjeeling's Goomtee Tea Estate looks happy and comes well-dressed to work, wearing a large bindi on her forehead.

retired as a labourer in the tea gardens. She sounds happy, for he has received a handsome monetary compensation.

'My grandfather Rattan Singh, was brought by force from Jharkhand (earlier Bihar). The *thekedar* (overseer) used to steal people and bring them to the tea gardens. But we were kept well, as we got *dawa, atta, chawal, khana pakane ke liye lakdi bhi!* (Medicines, wheat, rice, firewood as well).'

Her father's job could have been transferred as *badli* to the next generation but she proudly declares that her brother prefers to work as an engineer in the factory as he is educated and well qualified.

Her parents have returned home to Assam although her aunt continues to work in the tea gardens. Roopali has no intention of going back as she and her husband make enough money in the city, and would rather open a tea stall than work in the tea garden. In the face of this changing profile, the tea industry is beset with serious labour shortages.

In South India where literacy rates are high, labourers prefer to seek employment in garment factories in the nearby Tamil Nadu cotton belt rather than the tea estates as the work is lighter and the wages higher.

Although mechanised plucking has been mooted to combat the difficulties of spiralling wage bills and the paucity of labour, studies have established that this cannot be the solution as it has an adverse impact on quality because the leaf can get bruised.

Shear plucking is sometimes being employed in South India and workers are especially taught to ensure selectivity, but there is no match for manual harvesting to produce a cup of good quality tea. Shear plucking has to be done carefully, so as not to bruise the leaf. Any damage to the leaf might mar the quality of that lot of tea.

FACING PAGE: Shear plucking is sometimes used in the tea gardens of South India to surmount labour problems.

ABOVE: [CLOCKWISE FROM TOP]

Tea workers scramble to the factory at the outbreak of a sudden shower working diligently, even during monsoon rain;

Gentle faces at the Kelagur Tea Factory.

Care for the Workforce

Since work on a tea plantation is such a labour intensive operation, clearly the workforce is the backbone of a tea plantation. Large tea companies recognise the value of their workers and have set up several philanthropic projects for social welfare and cultural development. McLeod Russel India Limited, with a workforce of more than 100,000 workers on their tea estates, has educational projects like the Assam Valley School, the Assam Valley Literary Awards and the Williamson Magor Scholarship Scheme. Among other activities, the Group supports a blind school with boarding facilities for underprivileged children in the Moran District.

Assam Company Limited runs 'The Star Fish Initiative Thare Machi', in collaboration with a UK-based NGO wherein women and young girls are counselled and educated in health, hygiene and HIV Aids awareness, with classes being held in a twenty-feet container that was shipped from the UK and installed at the Maijan Tea Estate in Dibrugarh.

Apeejay Tea has an artisan programme for the skills development of its tea factory workers besides a serious effort to create health awareness and provide education. In their Kanan Devan Hills Plantations in Munnar, the Tata Group runs organisations like 'Athulya',

which trains workers to create 'wealth from waste' and 'Aranya', where artisans are taught textile dyeing using vegetable dyes.

In recent years, there has been a paradigm shift by leading tea companies to take on increasing social and moral responsibility for protecting workers in this labour-intensive industry. India has become a prominent contributor in producing Fair Trade certified teas, whereby they are in compliance with the Fair Trade partnership that seeks respect for workers, based on dialogue and securing their rights while participating in international trade.

Similarly, many tea companies also meet compliance with Rainforest Alliance certification that is based on meeting internationally accredited ecological, social and economic standards.

According to Ashok Batra, Consultant, Sustainable Value Chains, India, about 72 million kilograms of tea were accorded this certification in 2013, and this figure is growing each month with a growing perception of these aspects.

Measures such as these are but a small step of humanity to alleviate harsh employment conditions. A workforce

of over two million is deployed to harvest the 159,190** tea estates across the tea belts in India. As may be the case in any mammoth enterprise, the tea business suffers at times from the malady of restive labour and political upheavals. However, this well-loved beverage owes gratitude to the assiduous worker, the hand that plucks the leaf.

FACING PAGE: Children at the Moran Blind School run by the Williamson Magor-McLeod Russel Group in Assam break into a touching song as they welcome visitors.

ABOVE: In Munnar, against the locale of the omnipresent tea gardens, the Tata Group runs DARE (Developmental Activities in Rehabilitation Education).

BELOW: Within the same compound, another unit, 'Aranya' where young artisans are taught the art of vegetable textile dyeing.

ABOVE: The gracious KDHP planter's bungalow in Munnar overlooks punctiliously tended gardens.
FACING PAGE: Planters' bungalows maintain their old-world ambience and remain unaffected by modernity.

THE PLANTER'S LIFE

'…in the cold weather I could grow English flowers and vegetables. During the rainy season though, we grew Indian flowers and vegetables…It was a marvellous life. We had our own ponies and cattle for milk, though monthly groceries came up from Calcutta by steamer—a three week journey!'

~ *Peter Pugh*

Try getting into a conversation with a retired estate manager, better known as a 'tea planter', and you will detect the animation in his voice. He unleashes a treasury of anecdotes about his 'plantation days', painting vivid pictures of his work, his bungalow, his tryst with wild animals, and his reckless times of enjoyment at the club.

Undoubtedly, his is a world unique and his job is a curious mix of agronomy, engineering and professional management, as field operations give way to the mechanics of a factory where a good quality output of tea will establish the reputation of his garden. However, his work horizon does not stop here. He must also possess heroic bravado to contend with dangerous predators like tigers, leopards and wild elephants that sometimes wander into the estates. One cannot forget that most of the gardens have been carved out from thick jungles.

Most of all, a planter has the complex task of being the keeper of the immense workforce that resides on the plantation. The concept of 'womb to tomb' by which the management assumes responsibility for the workers' needs from maternity to death, is perhaps unique only to India. In Sri Lanka, much of the onus for worker welfare rests on the state whereas in Kenya, plantation workers do not live on the gardens but report for work in the nature of any regular job.

The manager on an Indian tea estate, however, is wholly responsible for the personal welfare of his workers. In colloquial terms he is often called *maibaap*, or considered a father figure as he even acts as arbitrator for personal disputes, to the extent of offering *vichar* (advice) for marital disputes and tracking down runaway brides.

Those Were the Days

This magnanimous position of authority of the planters is also a chronicle of their lifestyle that developed in consonance with the evolutionary passage of British India tea. To begin with, during the pioneering days, their lives were certainly not enviable. They lived in makeshift huts, enduring all sorts of tropical hazards.

John Weatherstone quotes a rather pitiable entry from the diary of a young planter in his book, *The Early British Tea and Coffee Planters and their Way of Life: 1825–1900—The Pioneers,* (Weatherstone:1986): 'If a planter had a sensible cook boy who was skilful enough to keep his master's rice in an old sock hanging from a rafter where the rats could not get their teeth into it, he was fortunate.'

By the nineteenth century as the tea plantations became lucrative, the planters began to grow in stature, being referred to as *burra sahib* by the locals.

Being stalwarts of tradition, they continued to maintain the decorum of their British ways in their daily lives. Young planters would make a special trip back home to find a bride and bring their memsahibs to live on these faraway estates. Here, as though to compensate for their isolation, and taking benefit of the labour at hand, they basked in a personal lifestyle, being attended upon by

an entourage of staff who were expected to maintain impeccable protocol.

There were *chowkidar*s or guards, *malis* or gardeners, bearers and valets, each with their assigned tasks. The head cook or *khansama*, together with his *paaniwala*s or assistants could turn out authentic traditional English meals. As the staff were housed in the huge compounds of the bungalow, they never left service, sometimes retiring only to hand over the same tasks to the next generation.

Weatherstone's book includes another revealing quote:

'…Some cooks, however, would seem to a visitor to have been trained in The Ritz, so good were they, were it not known that pure repetition of the same meal over and over again, year after year had finally made perfect!'

Life for the memsahibs was however, difficult. Children were sent home to England for schooling at a young age. As it took six weeks to get a letter and three months to take a voyage, they grew up only knowing their guardians, while even for the parents, their offspring became virtual strangers.

The more enterprising wives, however, busied themselves, honing their talents or hosting visitors from

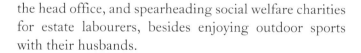

the head office, and spearheading social welfare charities for estate labourers, besides enjoying outdoor sports with their husbands.

For the planter, the day would begin at what in pidgin language, was known as *murghi dak* or 'at the crow of the rooster'. He would first ride out to the fields to ensure that the workers had started their plucking. After returning for an early breakfast, he would go for another mid-morning round in the gardens and the factory and meet the *sirdars* or supervisors who were on their toes, waiting for inspection.

Lunch time or tiffin was followed by a short siesta, usually stretched on a planter's chair on the airy veranda. As planters made an early morning start, these chairs were designed to provide them a comfortable recline for a post-lunch siesta, and the broad arms offered space for placing a drink while relaxing with the memsahib in the evening.

Then it was back to work in the office to deal with mail and paperwork to report to the bosses in Calcutta who, would, in turn send long reports to London. An account from the Goodricke Group's book, *Camellia: The Lawrie Inheritance* mentions that 'mountainous mail' had to be handled.

It goes on to say: 'The Calcutta partners wrote weekly to London. The style of writing was rigid and formal, such as "we beg to state" and "we beg to remain…" letters from Home were usually admonitory.' (Manton: 2000).

Evening was meant for a meeting with the managers and overseers to listen to complaints, to review the day's work, and plan for the next day. After sundown, it was time for a drink with the memsahib, or perhaps a game in the billiard room in the special outhouse for recreation, or simply for reading by a crackling fire in the spacious living room.

FACING PAGE: All India Rugger Tournament—Madras 1935 Planters vs Bengal Nagpur Railway, Munnar Tea Museum.
ABOVE: [CLOCKWISE FROM TOP LEFT] A narrow gauge railway that was pulled by light steam locomotives was introduced in Munnar in 1908 to transport tea from the hills to the southern plains; A *burra sahib* poses with his kill; Madras Rugby Tournament 1933 Planters vs Somerset Light Infantry, Munnar Tea Museum; Planters made the most of the jungle surroundings of their tea estates and enjoyed shikar.

FACING PAGE: Ready for lunch at Rossell Tea's Dikom Tea Estate in Assam.

ABOVE: A heritage post box in Darjeeling.

ABOVE: An estate manager and his wife relax over a cup of tea in their heritage bungalow at Nonsuch Tea Estate, Coonoor. The colourful country-style padded sofas combine with a brilliant hand-embroidered Indian wall-piece. The décor represents a mix of the bygone with the present, the essence of a planter's lifestyle today.

ABOVE: [CLOCKWISE FROM TOP LEFT]
The Planter's bungalow at McLeod Russel India Limited's Sepon Tea Estate, a classic haven of the past;
The charm of a planter's living room, complete with a fireplace;
Planters in animated conversation at the Moran Tea Estate.

Nostalgia Lingers On

Today, especially in the larger companies, planters continue with a similar lifestyle and their staff operates much the same way. Bearers still lay out the perfect table, complete with starched napkins and lace doilies. They glide into the dining room, silently serving dishes at your elbow and placing finger bowls at the end of the meal. Ramdin, the cook, proudly tells you that his grandfather had presided over this very kitchen in 'those' days. He turns out roast meat and potatoes and a flawless caramel custard with the same aplomb as delectable Indian curries. The vegetables served are extraordinary for their freshness and flavour, as they are grown in the bungalow's backyard.

This plantation lifestyle simply lives on. The wives continue to play their role as gracious hostesses and carry out social welfare activities, making the most of their isolation and their children still have to be sent away to boarding schools.

The work routine of their husbands also remains much the same. Except, the jeep has replaced the horse, and reporting is to the bosses in their Kolkata offices. Communication channels such as the mobile phone, internet and satellite television are a boon of the present age. Still, as G.P. Goenka, Chairman of Duncan Tea puts it: 'I was working for a Scotsman fifty-nine years ago, when my father put me into the business. Nothing has changed. The same rituals carry on. A tea planter cannot fit into any other role in life.'

City life for a retired planter means a radical change that often fills him with yearning for a life of work and glory—days that he has left behind.

High Life and the Planter's Club

The most colourful facet of a planter's memories is the Planters' Club. This concept came into being as an outlet for planters to discuss and socially interact with each other to make up for their lonely tribulations in the estates.

The bar was the hub where they would begin their conversations, first by exchanging notes on the business affairs of their gardens, often venting frustrations over demanding directives from the London and Calcutta offices. A couple of drinks later, the mood would melt into frivolous camaraderie. Weekends were notorious for all-night drinking sessions and loud parties. The popular but heady cocktail called 'Planters' Punch' could possibly be a throwback to those rowdy evenings, as the word 'punch' is a derivative from the Hindi word *panch*, and the drink was originally made with five ingredients: rum, sugar, lemon, water and tea. Planters are happy to give accounts of rollicking escapades.

FACING PAGE: The photograph displays a planters' tradition that was curious to the High Range Club in Munnar. Their broad-brimmed sola topis were put up in the bar; only those with an unbroken service record of thirty years were accorded this privilege.

ABOVE: British planters in Assam learnt the game of Polo from Maharaja Chandrakii's players of the neighbouring kingdom of Manipur where it was known as '*Kanjai*'.

BELOW: Glimpses of a privileged life. Planters made the most of the great outdoors.

A recollection by a retired estate doctor in the Assam tea gardens: '…a good Samaritan (Peter Nag)…had his jeep with ropes and hook ready and spent quite a few nights hauling out the planters' cars from the ditches after a rowdy club night.' (*Contemporary Tea Time Vol. XIX No. 2*, June–August 2010).

Despite everything, the dress code and club etiquette were very important. Planters clad in breeches would arrive on horseback and then change into formals before ordering a cup of tea or the first drink of the evening. Women came attired in long skirts and were segregated in a separate lounge where they probably discussed the latest fashions in the catalogue order books from England, apart from having conversations centring on children, nannies and flowers in their gardens.

Every tea region had its own club. The Darjeeling Planters Club was established in 1868, and was once the centre of high society. The land for the Club building was donated by the Maharaja of Cooch Behar who earned the privilege of being the only person to be allowed to park his rickshaw in the main porch of the Club. It is said that sumptuous twelve-course dinners were held in the dining hall of the club on special occasions. Each table was identified by a flag that bore the name of its plantation. The finest English crockery and Belgian cut-glass were used, and fresh crockery was brought in from Calcutta for every celebration or event.

In Munnar, the High Range Club dates back to 1905. Its bar has an intriguing array of planters' hats or broad brimmed sola topis. Of these, forty-nine hats belong to Scotsmen and three to Indians of the later years. Only planters with an unbroken service of thirty years were accorded the honour of having their hats put up. The only exception was made for those who went away to serve in the war and came back to their life in the gardens. Young planters purchased these hats at Simon's Artz shop in Port Said when the ship carrying out from England docked en route at Aden before reaching India. It is said that those returning home threw away the topis into the sea as they crossed the port and headed out west towards the Mediterranean Sea. (Based on the account by Kenneth Warren, past Chairman, 1906–1923 Warren Tea Industries: Jones 1992).

Club life also laid great emphasis on outdoor sport. Hunting and fishing were particularly favoured. The game of Polo is said to be introduced by the tea planters of Assam who learnt it from the neighbouring players of the Manipur region during the reigning years of Maharaja Chandrakii, (1850–1886). The game evolved with the establishment of the Silchar Club at Cachar and in 1861, Assam Company became the first Company team to play a polo match.

So popular did the sport become, that Kenneth Warren once remarked: 'The obvious thing was to play polo. Everyone played polo and you were expected to, and if you didn't like it, well you'd jolly well got to lump it. I once had an assistant who came and said he didn't want to play, he wasn't keen on playing polo, so I told him, "Well, if you can't play polo you're not much use to me. I'll have to find somebody who can…"' (Pugh: 1991).

The Bar at the Wellington Gymkhana Club, Coonoor has a display of regimental rifles and shields. This Club was established in 1873, originally to provide recreation

Origin of a Great Game

By Compton Mackenzie

LAST year an article in " The Field " put forward the theory that the game of Snooker had its origin at the Royal Military Academy, Woolwich, where officers of the Royal Artillery and the Royal Engineers receive their training as cadets.

The theory was plausible, because a first-year cadet at " The Shop," as the R.M.A. is familiarly known, is called a " Snooker," the soubriquet being time's corruption of the original word for a newly-joined cadet, which was " Neux." It must be remembered that the R.M.A. was founded as long ago as 1741.

The writer of the article stated that the original rules of Snooker were copied out by Lord Kitchener from those at " The Shop," brought by him to Ootacamund, and there hung up in the Club.

This assertion was formally contradicted by General Sir Ian Hamilton in a letter to " The Field " of July 11th, 1938. In point of fact Lord Kitchener never visited India until many years after Snooker had become a popular game

Here, for the first time, is the fully authenticated story of the origin of Snooker.

It is presented by one of the most brilliant writers of our time, Mr. Compton Mackenzie.

This historic article, which could never have been written without the co-operation of Colonel Sir Neville Chamberlain, is proudly published by us at a time when the game itself is being played in Great Britain by more people than is any other sport or game.

would be very appropriate to call the game snooker. The suggestion was adopted with enthusiasm and the game has been called Snooker ever since."

Potted himself

In 1876 Sir Neville Chamberlain left the Devons to join the Central India Horse, taking with him the new game. A year or two later came the Afghan War, a more serious potting game in which young Chamberlain was himself potted.

However, fortunately for himself and the great game

[...] that the professional must [...] who came out to Calcutta in [...] that he remembered showing [...] of Snooker at Cooch Behar [...] spring of 1884.

Famous people r[...]

Sir Neville Chamberlain ha[...] distinguished authorities con[...] the inventor of Snooker. M[...] Colonel of the Central Indi[...] wrote:

" I have a clear recollectio[...] ment in 1884. You brought [...] which you called Snooker or [...] black, the pink, the yellow an[...] stood it was your own inven[...] keenly."

Major-General Sir John Ha[...] the 43rd Oxfordshire and Buc[...] wrote:

" I was always under the im[...] the game of Snooker to the 43[...] 43rd never played Snooker til[...] it to us. Hope you will st[...] invention."

Field Marshal Lord Birdwoo[...] " I remember well your intro[...] into the 12th Lancers' Mess, [...] the Regiment at Bangalore in [...]

Complete

Sir Walter Lawrence, Bt., wr[...]

Newspaper [...]reat to your [...]f "The Billiard [...]

by the well known [...] "Snooker". [...] at ootacamund

The Field, which (the Royal Academy al others), in the

he writer, but I that they [...] played at [...] of last century". [...]uest, and Compton [...] ish he had [...].J. Dunlop Watson, [...] follows:— [...] where I frequently

FACING PAGE Extract reproduced from a journal, 'The Billiard Player', April 1939.

ABOVE: The Darjeeling Planters' Club lounge was used primarily by the women.

BELOW: The game of snooker was invented in this historic Snooker Room at the Ooty Club.

for British garrison troops stationed here. Later, civilians and tea planters also became its members. Its military traditions however, continue and in the 1930s, the regimental band played music for weekly afternoon dances.

Similarly, 'snooker' is said to have been invented at the Ooty Club as it was here that Sir Neville Chamberlain, an officer of the British East India Company army, who was awarded the Order of the Star of India and was the Commander-in-Chief of the Madras Army from 1876–1881, drafted the first official set of rules for snooker in 1882.

The name 'snooker' was derived when Neville Chamberlain laughingly called a player who missed a shot, a 'real snooker'. The word, in those days, was used as a slang term for a first year cadet.

The Club was being initially founded for officers of the Madras and Bombay regiments, but it also came to include planters as its objectives were to offer something, 'to the numerous sufferers from the effects of a tropical climate, a substitute for those comforts and conveniences otherwise only procurable in their native land...' (Extract from a circular dated January 1, 1842, by Dr Baikie: Ootacamund Club). This spelt the philosophy

of the club culture that the British brought into India.

The boom in the tea business during the turn of the century gave the planters handsome benefits and salaries, so they could afford the luxury of affording fancy motor cars. In their position, they could even get away with some irrational fun.

'The legendary Reggie Gibbons drove a car down the length of Chowringhee in the rush hour against time for a wager. He pretended to be a fire engine. A coat of red paint, a ladder and a hand bell and the bet was won...' Extract from the book, *The Merchant Prince* by Sir Owain Jenkins, ex-Managing Director, Balmer & Lawrie. (Pugh: 1991).

Planters' Clubs remain preserved as a leaf of history and their interiors maintain the ambience of the past. They have parquet floors, old fashioned sofas and armchairs with a fireplace, trophies of boar and bison heads, photographs of tournaments won or of proud hunting parties celebrating their kill. The tradition of

the Hunt is of course long gone, in view of wildlife preservation. Indoor and outdoor sports facilities, like billiards, squash, tennis, badminton and swimming are still the mainstay of recreation for planters and their families. Many a planter boasts of a great golf handicap. Weekend fun and festive celebrations when wives organise elaborate dinners and dances are the highpoint of club life. It is a strong fraternity, a kinship borne out of their extraordinary lifestyle that is a paradoxical mix of hardship and luxury.

FACING PAGE BELOW: The bar in the Darjeeling Planters' Club.
ABOVE: The Bar at the Wellington Gymkhana Club, Coonoor has a display of regimental rifles and shields.

ABOVE: A close look at the withered leaf.

FACING PAGE: Plucking is the first and most vital stage of tea manufacture.

FROM NATURE TO MAN

'The best quality tea must have creases like the leathern boot of Tartar horsemen, curl like the dewlap of a mighty bullock, unfold like a mist rising out of a ravine, gleam like a lake touched by a zephyr, and be wet and soft like fine earth newly-dug.'

~ Lu Yu

The young buds and their tender leaves which are plucked from the gardens so painstakingly eventually acquire a new avatar, a rebirth, as the familiar twisted dry black, brown or green tea leaves which, when steeped in hot water, unfurl in a silent pantomime to release their gentle aromas, with hues that range from pale gold to coppery red, to delicate shades of green.

This near mystic transformation depends on the variety of leaf planted in the estate, and then the intervention of mind and hand in the manufacturing process, during which distinct changes in the physical and biochemical composition of the leaves take place.

Basically, production of black tea aims at breaking up the cells of the leaf, allowing the different chemicals in the leaf to interact with each other in the presence of oxygen, and then halting this process by subjecting the fermented leaf to hot air in specially designed ovens or dryers. The art of good tea manufacture is to know when to stop the fermentation, and then to dry the leaf to just the right degree. This calls for an intelligent evaluation of the ever-changing and variable ambient conditions that will influence what happens to the leaf at each stage of production.

Manufacturing Systems

Manufacturing systems are of three main types: the first arrests oxidation of the green leaf as soon as it arrives in the factory and results in the production of green tea; the second permits partial oxidation to take place and the end result is Oolong; finally in the production of black teas, the leaf is allowed to fully oxidise and two sorts of teas are made: Orthodox, in which the end result looks like twisted long leaf, and CTC, meaning, Crush-Tear-and-Curl, whereby the tea leaves look like pellets, shot and tightly curled.

In the early days tea manufacture in India was a cumbersome and laborious process and the pioneers faced numerous difficulties.

To begin with, tea factories were made of bamboo, planks, stones and thatch. They were hot and hazardous because of the line of charcoal burning ovens which were used for firing.

The main factory of the Assam Company at Nazira with its thatched roof frequently caught fire. It was powered by giant water wheels and the little machinery that was available, was transported by bullock carts or at times, by wheeled trolleys that were pushed manually.

The first consignment of tea that was produced took a whole year to manufacture and transport to the auction room.

Nowadays the old production methods of tea appear antiquated like the yellowing pages of history. Present-day factories are bright and airy, gleaming with sophisticated machinery that is becoming computer controlled, and tea is produced in a green environment where the strictest hygiene and international HACCP (Hazard Analysis and Critical Control Points) safety standards are employed.

Segregating the Leaf

As a beginning to a successful output of processed tea, a planter tries to ensure that a uniform size of leaf is plucked for each particular round of production. Different *jats* or derivations of the tea plant and varying leaf sizes release aromas that differ from each other and can lower the quality of the entire batch of tea.

Gardens usually employ three-tiered trailers to carry the leaf from the field to the factory so that the tender shoots do not get bruised in transit.

A representative sample of the leaf on arrival at the factory is first weighed in a small hand scale that either has a weight made up of a predetermined number of five paisa coins or metal balls.

The leaf so measured is then segregated by the length of the shoots plucked which are then counted so as to arrive at an accurate estimation of the quality that has been harvested from the field.

A high percentage of 'two-leaves-and-a-bud' and soft tender leaves will enable the planter to manufacture a consistent 'lot' of tea, as these respond more or less evenly to the various processes that the particular consignment is subjected to during the course of manufacture.

In Assam, at Rossell Tea's Dikom Tea Estate, the endeavour is to achieve a uniform plucking standard of at least 65 per cent of good leaf. The leaf from this garden is processed by both the Orthodox and CTC method.

The Company has six estates that together produce approximately five million kg of black tea, of which Orthodox tea comprises the major component. Most of the produce is exported, although it also enjoys a niche domestic market.

FACING PAGE: [TOP] Plucked leaves brought in to the factory by mechanised means.
[BELOW] Checking the fine leaf count by the method of 'paisometeric'.

ABOVE: At Assam Company's Greenwood Tea Estate factory, as it has been a rainy day, the leaf is being withered by propelling warm air through fan burners.

Withering: The Essential Step

Be it Orthodox or CTC production, the leaves must first be withered. During this process physical and chemical changes take place in the green leaf. The idea is firstly, to reduce the moisture content in each leaf to make the leaf more malleable in the factory, and secondly, very similar to the process of marinating, to break down the complex mixture of chemical proteins and carbohydrates in the fresh leaf into simpler amino acids and sugars, which increase the concentration of caffeine and polyphenols in finished teas.

In the initial years the plucked shoots were simply withered, by spreading them on *tats*, hessian or wired shelves, in covered sheds open on all sides, called *chung* houses. Nowadays, withering is done by spreading out the leaves on trays placed on long rectangular boxes or troughs, through which controlled volumes of air are passed by way of large electric fans. The leaf can take anywhere between 12–20 hours to wither, depending on the thickness of the leaf spread and the temperature and humidity of the air passed, also depending on the weather conditions at that time.

In some factories, mostly in the hill plantations, these troughs are placed in closed lofts and withering is controlled by opening the windows and providing additional air movement through fans. In other cases, rotating perforated drums are used instead of troughs while in some instances mobile trolleys may be employed to carry the *tats* through a tunnel that is subjected to hot air blasts.

On occasions when moisture-filled ambient conditions prevail, warm air is distributed through burners at the end of fan propellers to wither the leaf. The thickness of the leaf spread and weather conditions ultimately influence the withering time.

In this manner, withering is controlled by the circulation of ambient air and by regulation of its temperature to encourage the leaf to release its inherent moisture.

Withering, therefore, is a matter of intelligent consideration of several factors. This essential step is very important, as ultimately, the right degree of withering will be instrumental in bringing about the necessary chemical changes and these in turn will determine the final quality of the tea.

Almost twenty-five to seventy per cent of the moisture, depending on the liquor attributes aimed at, is extracted from the leaves at this stage, making them soft and pliable for further processing.

FACING PAGE: Visitors at the Kanan Devan Tea Museum and factory in Munnar enjoy a look at the withering troughs.

ABOVE: Tea leaves are first subjected to maceration in a Rotor-vane, and from here they fall on to a CTC machine.

BELOW: Cleaning the leaf.

Rolling: The Twist for Flavour

Next, the leaves are rolled, so that the leaf cells rupture to release the juices that contain the catechins and enzymes. In this process, the leaf is also twisted to bring out the distinct flavours of the tea.

In the early days, rolling was done manually. A line of workers stood on either side of a long table, passing a bunch of leaves from man to man, until they reached the top of the table. They used both hands in a figure-of-eight motion.

So lengthy and laborious was this process that it set a planter in Cachar named Nelson thinking. He invented what came to be known as the Nelson Roller. Sujoy Gupta in his book, *Four Mangoe Lane: The First Address in Tea* describes the invention.

'…It occurred to him (Nelson) that if one table was turned upside down and put on top of another table and then was moved backwards and forwards with leaf between the two tables, the rolling action would be the same and quantities of leaf could be treated.

However, he realized that the leaf had to be contained in something to hold it together. So Nelson sent for his white drill trousers. He cut off the legs, filled them with leaf, tied up the ends, put the 'bags' between the two tables, sat some coolies on the top one to add weight and set the others to pull and shove the inverted table over the bottom one.' (Gupta: 2001).

The mechanised system of rolling uses the same principle. The leaves are fed through rollers into a machine that has a table and jacket that rotate in opposite directions, so in this manner, the leaves placed in the jacket are twisted and rolled in a movement that resembles hand rolling.

The finer processed leaves so rolled are then passed through a sieve to separate them from the leaves that did not get properly rolled and sized and need to be taken through the rolling machines once again.

The underlying concept in rolling is essentially to mechanically separate the bud, the first leaf, the second leaf and the longer leaf so that the different sizes of leaf can each be dealt with appropriately during the manufacture process.

The hugely popular 'CTC' teas are more often introduced into machines like the Rotor-vane which does not roll the leaf, but rather 'distorts' and reduces its size quickly. The leaf then goes through sets of three or more horizontal serrated rollers that are placed close together in tandem, revolving at unequal speeds, and in the process, they Crush, Tear and Curl the leaf. It is this process that gives such teas their derivative name.

Their final shape will be given by the machine and the leaves will emerge as tightly curled pellets. This method of production is much faster than the Orthodox rolling and twisting.

The goal is achieved in both these methods of production: the juices and enzymes originally separated in the cells of the leaf are now inter mixed. While Orthodox rolling can take up to three hours, it takes only ten minutes in CTC processing.

The product that emerges is different, and both these types of processes produce teas that emit a brew that is distinct in colour and character.

While production in Darjeeling is wholly Orthodox or green tea, teas in all other planting districts such as Assam, North Bengal, the Nilgiris and Kerala are mostly CTC, although some fine quality Orthodox and green teas are produced in these regions as well.

FACING PAGE: [TOP] At the Goomtee Tea Estate in Darjeeling, a rolling machine processes the famed 'Muscatel Valley' tea.
[BELOW] Continuous fermentation in progress, a system that has been developed with technical advances in production.

Fermentation for Colour

It is in the process of oxidation, or fermentation, as it is more usually referred to in the tea industry, that coloured compounds are formed that endow the leaf with its dark copper tone. The chlorophyll in the leaf must be broken down so that its polyphenols are oxidised in the presence of the enzymes and its tannins are released whereby it develops a distinct flavour. At the end of the fermentation, the leaves have acquired the familiar dark copper tone, derived from oxidation.

The leaves are spread out on the floor or on long tables for one to three hours in a cool, humidified atmosphere. Here again, the leaves must be exposed to just the right amount of fresh air, so the leaf is sized for uniformity, as larger shoots require longer aeration. The thickness of the spread is a matter of judgement and practical experience. Humidifiers are employed to blow in cold air which is regulated according to the outside weather conditions so as to provide a controlled humidity for the oxygen to act on the enzymes. It is important to know just when to stop the fermentation. At Makaibari Tea Estate in Darjeeling, owner Swaraj 'Rajah' Banerjee explains:

'Fermentation has its peaking cycles, it goes up and down. So we go by the release of its smell, or "take nose" every few minutes and go by what we sense. There is no fixed timing, and different seasons or flushes yield teas that ferment differently. At the end of the day, it is our speciality to follow the nose for fine tuning the flavours of our teas.'

The process is stopped usually at the second peak, and the damp leaf is taken immediately to the dryer. The right duration of oxidation is most important in the formation of many coloured and aromatic compounds. It actually creates the type of tea desired, and a poorly fermented tea can result in grassy flavours, while an over fermented tea may have undesirable winey flavours.

As the oxidised green leaf changes colour and takes on a copper red tone, workers often refer to the fermenting room as the *rang ghar* or 'colouring' room. In the pioneering days, the fermenting room was housed under a thatched roof and although cooler than the factory, it was even darker.

The cemented floor on which the leaf was spread would be slimy with stale juice, but at that time, there was an erroneous belief that the quality of the tea liquor was the result of its inherent virtue of ripe maturity, and did not really depend on the process of fermentation.

ABOVE: The dried leaf emerges from the dryers in its familiar dark form and is brought in conveyor belts to be sorted and sent to the Waterfall fanner for removing tea dust before being sent for packing.

ABOVE: A fibre extractor removes the woody fluff before the dried tea is sent for grading.

BELOW: Old tea-bush roots are recycled for fuelling furnaces that generate blasts of hot air required in various stages of manufacturing.

Drying: The Final Step

Compare this scenario with the sophisticated Fluid Bed Dryers at the McLeod Russel India Limited's Moran Tea Estate in Assam. Mechanised systems of air control and gas fired heaters blow hot air at temperatures ranging from 85° to 130°C (260°F), through the fermented leaves that are conveyed in chains within the dryers. So strong is the blast that the air sounds like water bubbles. This process stops oxidation and can take twenty to twenty-five minutes. At the end of it, the moisture content of the rolled and fermented leaves is only three per cent in the dried and finished black tea

and one can recognise the long leaf, or granules which are sold in the retail market to consumers. On the brink of being ready, the tea leaves are passed through one last dryer to ensure that no excess moisture has crept in during the interim stage before they are sent for packing.

Sorting & Grading for Quality

The end product of manufactured dry tea has to be sorted and separated into grades of different sizes. This is important, as blending mixed sizes of tea leaves would simply not produce the right quality of uniform

tea liquor. A flashback to the early days describes the sorting rooms which, although not as dark as the fermenting rooms, were filled with clouds of dusts from the sorters and cutters, and had no system of exhaust.

> 'The *Sirdar* in charge and other operatives took on a distinct yellow hue which they slowly lost in the months that ensued before starting the next season's manufacture.' (Androbus:1957).

Present-day factories have refined methods of sorting. Conveyor belts take the leaf to a pre-sorter, which is a hopper with a mesh that separates the bigger leaves, and also passes them over magnetic rollers that remove

the fibre extracts. Next, there is a principal sorter in which the hopper sorts the leaf into three main grades, known in tea terminology as 'broken', 'fannings' and 'dust'. Broken grades are again sorted through meshed 'googies' for premium and secondary grading. The grade nomenclature does not reflect quality, it merely indicates leaf size.

FACING PAGE A sophisticated computerised colour-sorting machine is fitted with sensors that separate the stalk from the leaf in the dried tea.
ABOVE: On the brink of being ready, the tea leaves are passed through one last dryer.
OVERLEAF: Women in a tea factory in Assam pick out foreign particles and left over stalks by hand.

Packing: Set for the Market

The final challenge is to pack the ready tea in a manner that there is no invasion of moisture, which is the greatest 'enemy' of tea as it will result in a rapid degeneration of flavour. The finished product must therefore be handled quickly and the packing must be airtight, for there could be a long waiting period before the tea finally reaches the market. For instance, a 'second flush' tea plucked in May or June may not come up for consumption till December or later, not to mention the long journeys of the product if it is exported.

At first, teas were packed in wooden chests. Nowadays, tea is mostly packed in strong paper sacks. Jute bags and woven sacks made of High Density Poly Propylene (HDPP) are also used, especially for resale in the domestic market in India. Top quality CTC teas meant for export are sometimes vacuum packed so as to retain freshness and quality indefinitely.

Although laborious manual methods are now outdated, the man behind the machine continues to be of great relevance. This is so because, at every stage of production, it is the interplay of ambient air that plays a critical role, and it is important that the machines that conduct air are managed accordingly. There is no fixed formula. It is an innate feel for the leaf that must be translated within the framework of prevailing weather conditions to produce manufactured tea. The leaf responds to the treatment meted out to it.

As Krishan Katyal, Chairman and Managing Director, J. Thomas and Company, a leading tea auctioneering house in Kolkata, puts it: 'In the final analysis, it is the human element that counts. The tea bud is malleable and volatile. You slap it, it falls down. You stroke it, it smiles!' Here, then, lies the intrinsic relationship between nature and man.

FACING PAGE: A worker at the Kelagur Tea Estate in Chikmagalur is happy to pose before packages of bulk CTC tea.

ABOVE: [CLOCKWISE FROM TOP LEFT]

The sheer volume of bulk tea in the mammoth paper sack can be gauged as a visitor to a tea factory poses by its side;

A plaque at Moran Tea Estate factory pays tribute to the memorable services of a factory engineer;

Millions of kilograms of bulk tea are packaged and ready for export at a Harrisons Malayalam Limited factory in South India.

THE TEA TASTER'S VERDICT

'…smell and taste are in fact but a single composite sense, whose laboratory is the mouth and its chimney the nose…'

~ Anthelme Brillat-Savarin

The journey of the tea leaf from the garden to the cup cannot be complete until the tea taster gives his final verdict and identifies the quality of the end product. His is the last word on the subtle distinctions between ordinary, fine and superlative teas. This, however, is no regular 'tasting'. It is an act of skilled professionalism and it would have taken a tea taster at least five years of training to earn his position. Only then would he have gained enough knowledge to be able to perceive the entire composition of the tea he tastes, right from its growing conditions to detecting the flaws, if any, in its processing. His task is not just to appreciate the tea but to critically analyse it.

The tea taster dons an apron and commences his work. He looks more like a technician in a laboratory. For, he is going to perform an analytical task that is almost clinical in nature. A long table is set up preferably bathed in natural north light, and the porcelain tasting bowls are put out serially in rows, accompanied by pots that have a matching lid. The dry leaf, infused leaf and brewed tea are viewed and tasted one after the other, so that each stage of tea brewing can be gauged separately. The taster will first assess the visual appearance of the leaf and press it in his hand to check for freshness. He may also assess the leaves by smelling them, usually warming some in the hand, then exhaling into them to moisten them, and finally inhaling the aroma.

FACING PAGE: Master tea taster Sanjay Kapur, engaged at his San-Cha Tea Gallery, New Delhi.

Tea Tasting Session

An assistant teaboy moves along the length of the table with a hand scale to measure out the dry leaves, 2.5 grams, or 3 grams with precision and places them in the pot. A second teaboy follows, carrying a kettle with water that has been heated properly to a full boil. He pours the water over the leaves, carefully timing the brew for five minutes. The brewed tea is then poured into the tasting cups, allowing the taster to study the 'agony' or the unfolding of the leaves in the boiling water. Next comes the actual tasting, a process very similar to wine tasting. The taster takes in a few sips of the tea making distinct sucking sounds and rolls the liquid around in his mouth, as he mentally assesses the tea and then quickly spits it out into a spittoon. 'You stream it over your tongue to cover the taste buds, then roll it at the back of the palate to fully assess the sensory impact,' explains Arindam Mukherjee, Senior Manager, Marketing, who is busy tasting a consignment of tea that has come in from the gardens of Apeejay Tea to their Kolkata offices, before it is sent for packaging.

As the tea taster moves along the rows of cups, he dictates his observations to an assistant in a typical tea vocabulary, which is similar to the descriptive terms used by wine tasters and coffee tasters. Terms like 'stylish' apply to a superior dry leaf appearance, 'acceptable' may have some flaws, while 'whiskery' would be taboo to

buyers as it denotes some fibre content. The infused leaf may be described in words like 'bright', 'coppery', 'dull' or 'even' to denote the colour.

The terms used for the brewed tea liquor are even more descriptive. 'Body', denotes a liquor with fullness and strength. 'Character', which is a most desirable quality, also encompasses an acknowledgement of the origin of the tea. A 'bright cream' obtained on cooling of the tea indicates a well manufactured leaf. A 'fruity' taste, results from over-fermentation, and 'burnt' is undesirable as it occurs from extremely high temperatures during firing. 'Flat' would mean lacking in briskness because of faulty manufacture or storage.

The correct sorting and grading of tea is also evaluated. If the leaf is choppy or uneven, or too big for the grade size, it will affect the quality of the tea. Short cool withers and under rolling will cause the tea to be 'flaky'. 'Grassy' is also caused by a low plucking standard, as are 'washy' and 'weak'.

Similarly in the tea gardens, a planter can review the entire spectrum of activity that happened during the day by simply tasting the tea produced in his factory. At the Goomtee Tea Estate in Darjeeling, it is 5:00 p.m.

and Ashok Kumar strides into his office purposefully. He has just flown in from Kolkata and he is anxious to know about the standards of the tea that was made in his factory during his absence.

He heads to the tasting table in his office, and as he deftly sucks, rolls and spits out the samples. He not only points out the deficiencies in the plucking standards, but he also compares one 'lot' of tea with the other. 'Evaluating the tea is based on a palate memory of taste', says he, 'you simply tease out the qualities of the tea in your mind.'

Be it any tea factory, a tea tasting table is always a part of the manager or proprietor's office. If the consignment is to be directly sold to the buyer, it would be subject to another tea tasting by the vendee before he places his order.

If it is sent to an auctioneering house, they will conduct their own tea tasting for preparing the catalogue and there again, the buyer's representative would carry out his personal evaluation. The tea then would have been tasted several times over before it finally makes its way to the market shelves.

PAGES 206–207: A tea tasting session in progress at J. Thomas & Company, the largest and oldest existing tea auctioneer in the world, based in Kolkata, India's tea-capital. Rows of tasting cups as far as the eye can see.

FACING PAGE: An assistant moves along the line of mugs and pours hot water that has reached a full boil over a measured amount of tea leaves.

ABOVE: The taster samples each cup and mentally gauges the sensory impact of the sampled tea.

Blends and the Tea Taster

Basically, since tea quality is a highly variable commodity, it is necessary to market it as a standardised product. No two invoices of tea, even though produced and manufactured from the same tea estate on the same day are exactly alike. The same tea factory can produce an excellent quality tea from one trough of green leaf at say, 9:00 a.m. and by 11:00 a.m. produce a totally different quality from another trough.

To surmount these multiple variables, the art of blending comes into play. Different teas interact with each other much in the same manner as spices do for different curries, hence the buyer can blend different varieties of teas in a manner so as to achieve a consistent quality that can be replicated to assume a particular brand name.

'This is where commercialism meets the fine art of tea tasting,' says Jeremy Sturges, Senior Tea Buyer/Blender of R. Twining and Co. As one of the world's oldest tea companies with a 300-year-old past, Twinings themselves have never owned a tea garden. They have simply excelled in creating and marketing their own range of packaged blends.

'I create saleable teas, not manufacture them. I write the blends, line by line. There is no ready reckoner for tea, you go by feel, touch and the senses,' Sturges goes on to say, as he relaxes in the veranda of the Chamong Group's heritage bungalow at Tumsong Tea Estate in Darjeeling. The hard negotiations that he had with his hosts during the day over the prices of tea which he proposes to buy for his company have given way to a feeling of ease as a light drizzle creates a soothing melody on the tiled roof of the bungalow.

Sturges comes to India regularly for sourcing tea, and his last visit took him to Assam. He selects teas from different gardens, some for body and others for colour, and thereafter develops a consistent formula, developing his own ratios for that particular blend to bring out a predominant flavour of the tea that will proclaim the marketed brand.

He has been a tea taster for twenty-one years, and he loves his job: 'You don't do it for a couple of years and leave it. You do it for a lifetime!'

The teas selected by master tasters like Sturges for the final blend are taken for assembly to the factory that is equipped with large drum blenders which mix the individual invoices to ensure that the end result is a thorough and consistent blend. Some brands may comprise blends of ten to thirty different teas. They may even combine teas from different countries, say, from India to China, mixing black tea with green, in a delicate fusion of full-bodied flavours with mild, so that the result is a tea whose origin cannot be pinpointed at all.

FACING PAGE Tea display at Twinings of London.

ABOVE: During the entire course of their long history, the iconic Twinings have never owned a tea garden.

BELOW: Twinings Tea-Bar has a sampling counter for tasting loose tea.

Marketing through Tea Auctions

Apart from private transactions, buyers can use the convenience of sourcing their teas from tea auctions. These are more like specialised supermarkets, where every conceivable quality and variety is available, so that the buyer can make his own selection through one point, the auctioneer acting as guarantor of this transaction.

As a natural outcome to their pioneering initiatives, the sale of tea by auction was also started by the British. The monopoly of the East India Company over commodities, including tea, drew voices of protest and it was suggested that the cargo should be disposed of by 'public outcry' at the auction rooms so that transactions were more transparent. The first such auction was conducted at the Company headquarters at Leadenhall Street in London in 1679. When, in 1834, the East India Company was divested of its commercial functions and tea became a free-trade commodity, an alternate location for the auctions had to be found. After a temporary venue in a dance academy hall in Change Alley, finally, Mincing Lane came to be a great auction centre. By now the tea trade was booming, and tea tasters would evaluate the samples from tea chests offloaded by clipper ships and record their findings in voluminous registers, often working through the night by candlelight.

Mincing Lane has been overrun by the turning wheels of time, having closed down in 1998. Kolkata now has the honour of having the world's oldest functional tea auction centre, J. Thomas & Company Private Limited, as it is called today, that dates back to more than 150 years. It began as a Welsh family-owned partnership commodities broker for items such as indigo, jute and shellac under the name of Thomas Marten & Company. At the time when it held its first tea auction on December 27, 1861, it was known as R. Thomas and Company, eventually adopting its present name by way of changing partnerships.

Nowadays, as private transactions and direct exports for the marketing of tea have become increasingly common, some of the older tea broking firms have not survived. J. Thomas however, holds its ground and takes the lead, handling more than 155 million kilograms of tea annually, nearly one-third of the tea auctioned in the country. They have a presence in all the major auction centres, namely, Kolkata, Guwahati, Siliguri, Jalpaiguri, Coimbatore, Coonoor and Kochi. Amritsar also hosts an auction centre that offers small quantities of green teas mostly from the nearby region of Kangra Valley.

PAGES 212–213: E-auctions developed in India under the auspices of the Tea Board.

FACING PAGE: Buyers at a tea auction by public outcry study the invoice numbers of the 'lots' of tea listed in the catalogue.

ABOVE: Keepsakes associated with tea auctions of bygone days.

BELOW: The ambience of the boardroom at J. Thomas & Co.

The Company's offices are located in a modern building called Nilhat House, meaning 'indigo market'—a name that represents its beginnings. The land on which it stands is itself a piece of history. Once the residence of General Clavering, a member of the Governor General's Council, its deed of sale was signed by Warren Hastings in 1778. The boardroom exudes the past with old photographs and dated bound records that reside in glass paned cupboards and memorabilia that take the visitor back to the days when pink gins were served during auction breaks.

This sort of tradition has long melted into the shadows, but the activity in the auction hall remains very much the same. Animated voices fill the room as buyers sit behind desks in amphitheatre style seating, vying for teas. All are intent on the main auctioneer who sits on the dais and calls out the 'lot' numbers of teas that have been listed in the catalogue with their Invoice numbers. The action is swift, as the auctioneer targets to sell four 'lots' a minute. The teas have their own invoice numbers and the quantity of tea under one 'lot' number could vary anywhere from 100 kilograms to 3,000 kilograms.

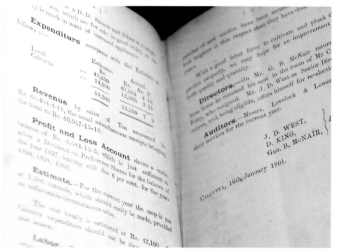

These auctions are held throughout the year and tea tasting for cataloguing is an exercise that is intrinsic to the daily work routine. A hierarchy of tasters do individual tastings to assess each category of tea and then compare notes to reach a common consensus.

As Gautom Chatterjee, Executive Director, of J. Thomas points out: 'In a typical day, we spend at least half a day tasting muster samples before dealing with daily sales of teas and back office documentation.'

He was once a second generation planter and now loves this dimension of his job. He often tastes one thousand cups of tea in a day. Together with his team, they put up the price ideas for the tea in the printed catalogue for the following week's auction. However, in this age of technology, tea auctions by public outcry are being superimposed by e-auctions, a concept that has been pioneered in India under the umbrella of the Tea Board. So successful is it proving to be, that its working is being examined by other major tea-auction centres such as Colombo, Sri Lanka and Mombasa, East Africa.

The e-auction room is charged with concentration, as the buyer focuses on the desktop screen before him. He watches the bids change colour while indicating the current position. All he must to do to compete against a bid is to merely click the mouse of his computer. Remote buyers stand to great gain as they can participate in these e-auctions by simply going online.

At the end of it all, despite these strides in super technology, effectively, the brightly packaged teas that are arrayed on the market shelves are the outcome of human inputs that are provided by the tea taster's discriminating evaluation.

FACING PAGE: [CLOCKWISE FROM TOP] Sepia memories of a tea auction; An entry in one of the tea reports, 1901; The present-day offices of J. Thomas & Co. stand on a land, the sale deed of which was signed by Warren Hastings in 1778.

ABOVE: The vocabulary that tea tasters employ to describe their observations resembles terms used by wine tasters.

OVERLEAF: The leaf, the brew, the packet: a close look at tea tasting.

TEA
THE **UNIVERSAL**
BREW

A cup of tea. That's all it is. But in the real sense, this everyday beverage deserves a position of honour in the culinary activity of the world. Savoured by all, it is unanimously agreed that this aromatic infusion, with its varying nuances of preparation, brings about a near magical transformation. It rejuvenates tired nerves and soothes the spirit into a sense of well-being. Notwithstanding nationality, language, caste, colour or creed, the love of tea is universal, stretching across almost all continents, in both northern and southern hemispheres. Moreover, the beverage is accredited with highly valued medicinal properties, much spoken of and widely researched in modern times.

FACING PAGE: Innumerable choices for the connoisseur.

ABOVE: An attractive display at a tea shop in Kunming, China. The discovery of tea has resulted in the production of exquisite tea accessories over the ages.

FACING PAGE: A Yixing pot with inscriptions in Chinese. Yixing pots were the first and foremost teaware made in China from the local *zhizha* clay. This pot dates back to somewhere around 1900.

THE SAGA OF TEA

'Wouldn't it be dreadful to live in a country where they didn't have tea?'

~ Noel Coward

Tea is a concoction steeped in history and traverses the passages of time, having given rise to some momentous global events. Wars have been fought, new countries born and several others brought to the international map by way of tea trade economies. Indigenous cultures have developed, based on the tea-drinking habits of different races and national styles of tea presentation. Beautiful art forms have evolved in the form of a wide range of accessories and the development of some exquisite workmanship on teaware.

Indeed, the ubiquitous cup of tea has been a strong player in the amphitheatre of the development of mankind.

The first whiff in china

It could be part legend, part history or true fact, but tea is believed to have been discovered in the Yunnan Province of ancient China in the year 2737 BC, at the time of the philosophical emperor, Shen Nung. Also known as the 'Divine Healer', and being of a finicky and scientific bent of mind, he insisted that his water be always boiled before drinking. On one of his outdoor excursions, while the emperor was resting under a tree, his servant was terrified to find that some dried leaves had blown into the cup of water that he had just boiled. However, to his amazement, the master, rather than being enraged, was examining, with interest, the hot water which had taken on a light golden colour, emitting a delicate aroma.

This then was the genesis of the drink that was to take the world by storm. Over the next three centuries, tea remained within the domain of China, known initially for its medicinal value and later evolving through dynasties both in the manner of drinking and presentation.

During the time of early Han Dynasty (AD 206–220 BC), tea preparation involved pounding a section of the roasted tea brick into small pieces and placing these in a china pot. Sometimes ginger, spices, orange peels and even onions were added before pouring boiling water over the tea pieces. The tea was drunk from the same bowls which were used for cooking and serving food.

By the fifth century, Turkish traders had started bartering with China for tea on the Mongolian border, and towards the end of the flourishing T'ang Dynasty (AD 618–906) tea trade with neighbouring India and Russia had also commenced along the Silk Route. It was during this era that tea came to be truly appreciated as a drink. Chinese farmers began to experiment with ways to develop its cultivation. For the first time, the leaves were turned into a powdered form, although tea bricks were still used. Tea drinking became a status symbol, a

matter of prestige, and imperial rulers used gold, silver or copper teaware, leading eventually to coloured glazes of browns, greens and blues. During this time, the poet Lu Yu was inspired to write *Ch'a Ching* the first ever book on tea, describing its cultivation, preparation and also the manner of drinking.

Came the opulent era of the Tsung Dynasty (AD 960–1280), when powdered tea prepared with a small bamboo whisk in shallow bowls was adopted as the norm. Artisans began to produce exquisite ceramic tea accessories in dark blue, brown and black glazes, and potters near Yixing developed utensils from local *zhizha* clay that would lead to the creation of teapots in the following years. It had also been noticed by now that there were differences in various tea varieties. Reportedly, Emperor Hui Tsung, a great tea enthusiast, invited noblemen to participate in tournaments at his court where they were challenged to identify the different types of tea. The emperor had his own 'Imperial plucking' methods from closely-guarded secret tea gardens for his personal choices of tea. So obsessed was he by his tea hobby, that he even failed to pay heed to the mounting aggressive inroads of the Mongols, who eventually overthrew his empire.

Tea, however, went into decline during the Yuan Dynasty (AD 1206–1368), when Genghis Khan and Kublai Khan conquered Chinese territories. It is said

that Marco Polo was not even introduced to the drink when he visited China.

The drink regained its popularity during the Ming Dynasty, (AD 1368–1644). Emperor Hung-wu decreed a new method of preparation in which whole tea leaves were steeped in water, bringing it closer to its contemporary form.

As this resulted in a paler liquid, light colour ceramics were developed, and white teaware became the hallmark of this period. Yixing teapots were now produced to perfection. These are prized by tea lovers even now, as the special mineral content and porous nature of the clay helps retain the character of tea.

Today, the art of preparing and serving tea, with its underlying Confucian, Taoist and Buddhist philosophies remains intrinsic to Chinese culture.

FACING PAGE LEFT: Chinese poet Lu Yu, author of *Cha Ching* the first book penned on tea.

FACING PAGE RIGHT: Packaged selection of Pu-erh or fermented teacakes, a speciality of Yunnan Province. In its earliest form, roasted tea bricks were pounded to make the brew.

ABOVE: A tea shop in Guangzhou. The world first learned about the beverage from China.

Tea Fervour Grips Japan

It was inevitable for the tea fervour to permeate through to Japan from neighbouring China. Sometime around the twelfth century, on a quest to learn Zen Buddhism, the Buddhist priest Yeisei made a trip to Tsung China where he realised that after drinking tea, he could meditate with more concentration. He therefore returned to Japan with tea seeds, which he planted on the grounds of his temple near Kyoto. Yeisei tried out different methods for brewing tea and finally settled for the Chinese whisked tea.

The Imperial household quickly took to the beverage and during the Muromachi period, (AD 1336–1573) tea became one of the most delicate art forms, and *Cha-no-yu* or the Tea Ceremony was adopted, which also borrowed from Tsung norms. Simultaneously, there was a production of fine ceramics as potters tried to imitate Chinese styles. The kilns of districts like Seto, Mino, Iga, Bizen, Shida-yaki and Tokoname came to be well recognised.

The ceremony however degenerated into a betting game for wealthy nobles for identifying various tea blends, until, in 1394, the priest prince Ikkyu tried to restore its original element of reverence. His student, Murata

Shuko (AD 1422–1502) became the first Japanese tea master to codify the rules for the ceremony, defining the equipage and detailing of the cabinet in which the tea items were to be kept.

Finally, during the Momoyama period, under the acclaimed tea master Sen no Rikyu (AD 1521–1591), the tea ceremony regained its stature so that even the warlords began to pause at tea houses before going into battle.

The great warrior and despot, Toyotomi Hideyoshi became one of the greatest patrons of the tea ceremony.

It is said that eventually Rikyu was ordered by Hideyoshi to commit suicide as the former's enemies created a conspiracy implying that the tea master was planning to poison Hideyoshi with a fatal potion mixed in the green tea. Kakuzo Okakura in *The Book of Tea* describes Rikyu's final day of reckoning.

'Rikiu invited his chief disciples to a last tea-ceremony. Soon the host enters the room. Each in turn is served with tea, and each in turn silently drains his cup, the host last of all…according to established etiquette, the chief guest now asks permission to examine the tea-equipage. Rikiu places the various articles before them… After all have expressed admiration of their beauty, Rikiu presents one of them to each of the assembled company as a souvenir.

The bowl alone he keeps.

'Never again shall this cup, polluted by the lips of misfortune, be used by man.'

He speaks, and breaks the vessel into fragments.'

FACING PAGE: Equipage for the Japanese tea ceremony.

ABOVE: Tea box containing *maccha* tea.

BELOW: A Tokonoma, a recessed alcove with a scroll and a flower arrangement sets the mood in a Japanese Tea Ceremony.

Tea Aroma Infuses Europe

Tea, it is believed, first crossed eastern realms to go westward sometime during the sixteenth century. A Venetian diplomat, Giovanni Battista Ramusio (AD 1485–1557), in his book, *Delle Navigatione et Viaggi* (Voyages and Travels) made a mention of *Chai Catai*, (Tea of China), being brought by a Persian trader, Hajji Mohammed, to Venice.

Tea drinking culture, however, came to Europe through the great seafarers of those times, the Portuguese and the Dutch. The Portuguese had first manoeuvred a foothold in Macau, during the T'ang Dynasty, to establish a monopoly on the trade between China and Japan. This gave an opportunity for Jesuit priests to traverse the seas to spread their religion. Jaspar de Cruz, a Catholic priest, who visited the Cambodian king's court in 1555, was the first to mention tea, when he wrote a letter back home. The Portuguese began to ship tea to Lisbon, from where it was transported to European and Baltic countries by Dutch ships.

Gradually Holland broke its affiliation with Portugal, and started independent trade, by establishing the Dutch East India Company in 1602, based in the city of Batavia, now Jakarta, Indonesia. Dutch ships began to trade sage with the Chinese in exchange for tea. The first consignment of tea arrived in Holland in 1610.

Since the drink was a new and strange commodity in The Hague, it was exorbitantly priced, at more than $100 a pound. It was a drink only the rich could afford. It also created a stir in society, giving rise to 'tea heretics', or the intelligentsia, who had heated discussions on the negative and positive effects of tea-drinking. Dutch inns and taverns started offering a special tea service in their gardens with a portable tea set and a heating unit so that guests could brew their own tea. It is believed that it was the Dutch who introduced the concept of steeping tea leaves for five minutes and using a tea cosy to protect the teapot.

LEFT: Giovanni Battista Ramusio's book, *Delle Navigatione et Viaggi* ('Voyages and Travels').

RIGHT: A picture postcard—a reproduction of a sixteenth century Dutch tea tavern.

ABOVE: A Salon de thé in the heart of St. Emilion, Paris. France continues with the tradition of tea.

BELOW: A tea shop in Hamburg exhibits a well-stocked selection of teas from around the world.

French high society also took to tea around the same time. It had arrived in France in 1636, twenty-two years before it would reach England. King Louis XIV, as well as his trusted advisor, Cardinal Mazarin, are both said to have been tea drinkers. The social critic, the Marquise de Sevigne, made the first mention of tea in 1680 when she wrote in a letter that she had seen a certain Madame de la Sabliere add milk to tea, a habit which would later be adopted by the British.

Tea could have impacted the French Revolution, as it was considered elitist taken as it was, with accompaniments like cakes, pastries and other delicacies even while the common man was groaning under the weight of high taxes and food shortages. The tea fashion, as a consequence, died down soon after the Revolution. Fifty years later, when tea became a habit in England, France too saw a revival of the tea-drinking habit.

The French had started with importing teaware from China along with the tea, but around 1735, a Jesuit priest, Francis Xavier d' Entrecolles brought back with him, the Chinese secrets of manufacturing porcelain. Soon gifted potters from Vincennes commenced the creation of exquisite porcelain for royalty that also included teaware. The factory moved to Sevres in 1756, and it soon became the designated manufacturer of porcelain for the Court.

In neighbouring Germany, tea drinking first became popular in OstFriesland in the lower Saxony district, through the North Sea route. By 1710, exquisite hard paste porcelain including delicate teaware was being produced in Meissen near Dresden and came to be recognised in Europe with its trademark logo of the crossed swords. Much later, in 1891, Rosenthal, another German company, would establish its name in fine porcelain.

Even today the port of Hamburg is a leading European centre for the international tea trade, with the main European wholesalers in tea being based here. Shipments of teas are imported and blended before being re-exported to global markets. In particular, Germany remains a key buyer for Darjeeling tea from India.

FACING PAGE: [TOP] A teapot from the house of Meissen, a pioneer in the manufature of teaware in Germany.

[BELOW] A classic Wedgeweood tea set from England.

ABOVE: A Wedgewood Tea set. Wedgewood was one of the first companies in England to manufacture elegant teaware.

BELOW: Sevres teapot from France.

The English Cup of Tea

The British romance with tea has propelled many historical events and created social customs that are woven into the fabric of contemporary society. The beverage, however, made its appearance in England relatively late, during the mid-seventeenth century, making it the last of the three great sea-faring nations to break into the Chinese and East Indian trade routes.

By this time coffee was already an accepted drink and in 1657 Thomas Garraway, a coffee merchant, ventured to sell both liquid and dry tea in his coffee house, extolling its virtues and health benefits. By 1700 there were several coffee houses selling tea. Exclusively for men, these came to be called 'Penny Universities' because for a penny any man could obtain a pot of tea and a copy of the newspaper while enjoying a witty exchange with his friends and colleagues. Various coffee houses had gatherings of men of specialised business, such as attorneys, authors, the military, etc. One such beverage house was owned by Edward Lloyd who started his enterprise in London as a beverage house owner where ship merchants and marine insurers gathered over tea.

This eventually led to the origin of Lloyd's, a reckoned name in global insurance.

After the catastrophic Great Plague of 1665 and the Great Fire of London, tea gardens like Vauxhall and Ranelagh opened in the suburbs of the city on the same lines as the Dutch tavern gardens. They were well favoured, knowing for a fact that tea was a safe beverage as water had to be boiled for its preparation. Women could now enter a mixed public gathering for the first time. During weekends the entertainment package included the service of tea, as it was considered a safe beverage, it being a known fact that water had to be boiled for its preparation. Some historians mention that it was at such a Tea Garden that Lord Nelson, the great British Admiral who defeated Napoleon at sea, used to meet his lover, the beautiful Emma, Lady Hamilton.

These tea gardens also gave rise to the social norm of tipping. Small, locked wooden boxes were placed on the tables on which were inscribed the letters T.I.P.S., meaning, 'To Insure Prompt Service'. A guest simply dropped a coin into the box on being seated and the waiter would give him an extra quick service.

A new addition to the English language may be attributed to tea. The word 'teetotal' could have an interesting derivative from the course of tea history, as, during this period, this beverage began to play an important role in the temperance movement's battle against the consumption of very high levels of alcohol, particularly gin. Tea meetings were held all over Britain in an attempt to convert drinkers and to raise money for the cause. It is believed that this may have given rise to the word 'teetotaler', one who abstains from alcohol.

China teaware had become a feature of every aristocratic and middle class English home. The Chinese drank tea in small bowl-like cups, but the British preferred cups with handles. They created their own pottery industry and companies—Spode, Wedgewood and Royal Doulton—that developed elegant crockery came to be established and are well known as reputed teaware producers to this day.

LEFT: Sir Thomas J. Lipton, pioneer of the world famous Lipton brand.
FACING PAGE: [TOP] A Twinings delivery van, 1956. Twinings is the oldest existing company that has traded continuously on the same site.

The introduction of 'clipper ships' gave a further boost to the drink by way of increasing the tea trade. Originally designed in the 1800s by the Americans, these streamlined vessels with tall masts could easily outstrip the heavier 'tea wagons' and travel at greater speeds than ever before. A journey from London to Hong Kong that earlier took over a year, could now be undertaken in as short a period as ninety-five days. This led to competitive 'clipper races', where ships would vie with each other to reach the London docks and unload their cargo first to earn a reward.

One of the best known clipper ships was the 'Cutty Sark', built by a Glasgow-based Scottish company, which, having lost its rudder during the race of 1872, still made it back to Canary Wharf in London on an improvised rudder in just 122 days.

By this time, the John Company had merged with the East India Company that had been instrumental in establishing tea plantations in India. The increased demand for the beverage was now encouraging imports from both China as well as India, and several enterprising tea merchants began to have flourishing businesses. One such entrepreneur was Thomas Twining. He moved from his village of Twyning, near

CENTRE: A tea garden in England. After the Great Plague of 1665, tea gardens and taverns opened around London on the same lines as the Dutch taverns.

BELOW: Doorway to the Twinings Museum & Shop, London, erected in 1787. The Golden Lion and two Chinese figures were built by Richard Twining, grandson of Thomas Twining, in 1787.

Gloucestershire, leaving his family business of weaving and wool processing, and arrived in London as a young man of twenty-six, where he started working with an East India Company tea merchant. By 1706, he had taken over Tom's Coffee House at The Strand and set up his own business. The Twinings address remains the same, and the company has a worldwide distribution network of its well-known brands of packaged teas and coffees.

After the success of tea in India, the British turned their attention to Ceylon, now Sri Lanka. This was much later in 1887, when James Taylor chose to undertake tea cultivation after a blight struck his coffee estate in Loolecondera.

In 1890, an Irish immigrant grocer who had grown up in the slums of Glasgow, having gathered retailing skills in his family store, as well as experiences in America that had made him a man of substantial wealth, stopped by in Ceylon on a holiday passage to Australia. He made good the opportunity to buy four such estates for furthering his business of tea. This was Thomas Lipton, and his brand name under the global Unilever Group remains an icon in the world of tea even today.

ABOVE: Fast sailing clipper ships heightened tea trade, giving a fillip to the popularity of tea.
BELOW: A Wedgeweood tea set.

Tea Shapes American History

The Dutch, under Peter Stuyvesant, the last Director-General of the Settlement of New Amsterdam initially brought tea across the Atlantic in 1650. Later, in 1664, New Amsterdam would be ceded provisionally to the English, and be known by the name it is known to the world today—New York City.

It was only a matter of time before the first tea gardens were opened in the city, located mostly around natural springs and soon enough there was a tea craze. By 1710, the wealthy colonists in Philadelphia and Boston began to consider the drink as a sign of sophistication. Elaborate tea parties with expensive teaware became the symbol of social success. The Puritans liked to drink bitter tea with butter and salt, while New Englanders preferred green China tea scented with saffron and gardenia petals.

Tea became the biggest trade commodity between America and England. Meanwhile the Crown began to feel the financial crunch of the war which they had fought to free the colony from French influence and stabilise trade. In a bid to generate funds, the Townshend Revenue Act of 1767 placed a heavy tax on tea. Strong protests against this measure led to a boycott of tea and in the bargain, stoked the fires of the breakaway from the control of the mother country.

The climax came on December 16, 1773, when patriots from Saint Andrew's Masonic Lodge, dressed as Indians (as a throwback to the French–Indian war) boarded the ships in Boston, and dumped 340 chests of tea into the harbour. Thus, *the Boston Tea Party*, as it came to be known, became the springboard for the American War of Independence.

Culturally, the credit of introducing the concept of iced tea to the world goes to the Americans. Some claim that eighteenth century southern cookbooks mention the preparation of iced tea in the form of punches made with green leaves as by that time refrigeration had been invented. However, iced tea in its present form was really popularised by Richard Blechynden at the 1904 St. Louis World Fair that took place on a blistering summer day.

As Commissioner for Tea in India and in-charge of the East India Pavilion, seeing that buyers were feeling too hot to try out his free samples of the beverage, he dumped a whole lot of ice into the tea and so created one of the world's most marketable drinks—iced tea. The

first large shop to sell tea opened in 1859, in New York, as the Great American Tea Co. store, at the initiative of a young local merchant, George Huntington Hartford, who persuaded his employer George P. Gilman to give up his hide and leather business. Hartford and Gilman bought whole clipper ship cargoes in New York harbour, and sold the tea at less than one-third the price charged by other merchants. This was the beginning of the A & P retail food chain.

Four years later, Thomas Sullivan, a tea and coffee merchandiser from the Big Apple (New York) unwittingly introduced the tea bag. Instead of deploying pricey tins for sending loose tea samples to restaurants, he experimented with using small silk sacks. Potential clients, nonplussed by this new packaging, threw in the sacks, as they were, in hot water. Sullivan was shrewd enough to realise that the restaurants were continuing to brew the samples in this form simply to avoid the mess of cleaning up tea leaves in the kitchens. So he purposefully commenced the development of sachets made of gauze for better steeping of tea leaves. Later, Thomas J. Lipton designed the multilateral tea bag seen today.

ABOVE: Boston Tea Party. This momentous protest against England's heavy taxes on tea effectively triggered the American War of Independence.

OVERLEAF: Commensurate with the many choices of tea, kettles and teapots come in a variety of shapes and forms.

The World in a Teacup

Over the ages, tea drinking, as a habit, has permeated almost the entire world. In eastern lands like China, Japan and Korea, the brew still carries its aura of philosophic origins with tea ceremonies that are conducted as art forms. Influenced by their own peculiar history, several of the countries in fact, have developed their own cultural nuances that are associated with the beverage.

So too, the brew has influenced the creation of some beautiful teaware across the world. It is believed that to begin with, the first kettles were said to have been used in Mesopotamia, between 3500 and 2000 BC, possibly for cooking, rather than boiling. Over passing time, the brew has inspired the development of chinaware and delicate porcelain so imaginative and intricately decorative that certain tea accessories can rank as collectors' items.

Tea, therefore, has played its role in giving rise to splendid craftsmanship, besides shaping lifestyles and creating landmark customs.

ABOVE: A row of earthen teaware displayed in a tea shop in Singapore; Chinese influence created a strong tea drinking culture in the region.
FACING PAGE: Variety of exquisite teaware from a private collection.

Tea Ceremony in China

The art of preparing and serving tea, with its underlying philosophies, remains intrinsic to Chinese culture. The hostess in a Chinese tea ceremony conveys these values through delicate hand movements and facial expressions.

She may employ the *Gongfu Cha* method: A clay teapot and bowls are rinsed and placed on a special tray that provides for drainage of water spillage during the course of the tea preparation. One-third of the pot is filled with tea leaves and hot water poured over them to the point of overflow.

The pot is then drained, boiling water is poured once again over the residue of wet leaves and the lid of the teapot is closed for thirty seconds. The aroma of the tea is further sealed by pouring more hot water over the closed pot. It is now ready to be dispensed into the cups.

Sometimes the tea may be prepared in the same manner in a *gaiwan* or wide bowl that is covered with a lid through which the infusion is slipped through to be poured into the cups. Several infusions can be derived from the same tea leaves. In essence, tea, for the Chinese, is a drink to be had throughout the day.

ABOVE: A hostess in a tea shop in China prepares tea the traditional Chinese way in a Gaiwan.
FACING PAGE: [CLOCKWISE FROM TOP LEFT]
A compressed teacake; Way to hold a teacake;
The spirit of tranquility with which the tea is to be enjoyed;
The delicate style in which women must hold a cup in the Chinese tea ceremony;
The style in which men must hold it.

Tea Ceremony of Japan

Despite Japan's leap to technology, Sen no Rikyu's traditions of *Cha-no-yu* are still alive, and remain a cultural hallmark of the country. The three main schools of the tea ceremony that exist today still proclaim their filial ties with the family name *Sen*— Omotesenke, Urasenke, and Mushanokojisenke. Mastering the fine art of the tea ceremony can take years to learn. Its rituals are both fascinating and meditative.

Take, for instance, Mrs Midori Uragami, a tea master of the Omotesenke School. She is a frail and gracious lady in her mid-eighties, who demonstrates the ceremony in her Tokyo home to her following of young students. Her four-and-half sized *tatami* tea room or *chashitsu* (in Japan, traditional room sizes go by the sections of a *tatami* or mat) is specifically measured. It has a *tokonoma*, a recessed alcove, with a beautifully calligraphic scroll and a *chabana*, a simple flower arrangement. Together, they depict a theme that usually represents a season.

In a corner stands the *daisu*, a double shelf display for the tea utensils. Here, Uragami-san sits in a typical *seiza* posture with legs folded under her knees, and heats the water in a *furogama* over a portable burner. She uses a *chashaku* to scoop a small amount of powdered *maccha* green tea in a bowl, pours water and whisks it with a bamboo *chasen* until it is thick and frothy. In winter the tea preparation may be shifted to a central portion of the *tatami* so that the iron pot sits inside a *ro* in the floor, a cut-out which serves as the hearth.

Uragami-san moves with experienced precision. Some of the tea bowls she uses may be priceless and hundreds of years old. Her collection could include *Wabi* style bowls that were introduced by Sen no Rikyu and these are usually irregular and simple in shape to represent beauty in austerity and imperfection. Other tea masters might use low fired unglazed *Raku* style bowls that are named after the great tea master Raku Chojiro (1516– 1592) and continue to be produced by the fifteenth generation of potters in and around Kyoto.

Guests must drink their tea in a particular manner. They turn their cup to take two-and-a-half sips, admire the cup, and wipe it clean to pass on to the next guest before it finally goes back to the host.

Uragami-*san* also has an outdoor tea house in her building compound. Although it seems simple in design, it is very expensive to fabricate, and is made entirely of interlocking wood, using no nails at all. It has an entrance so low that guests have to enter almost sliding in on their knees. It is not hard to imagine the haughty samurai of yore, unsheathing their swords at the entrance, entering in all humility. Women must stow away all their jewellery, so that inside the tea room, all are equal.

As a somewhat contemporary adaptation, at Rinko Okano's family temple, the Kodosan Temple in Yokohoma, the tea ceremony may also be conducted in the Ryurei style, where the host prepares tea at a special table. Larger ceremonial tea houses are set in beautiful natural forest surroundings with bamboo groves, pebbled paths, carp-filled ponds and wooden bridges. Guests immerse themselves in this serene environment, leaving behind the throbbing commercialism of the outside world.

Tea Drinking in Germany

OstFriesland in the lower Saxony district of Germany has the world's most impressive number of tea drinkers. Typically, Frieslanders prepare a strong black tea that is a blend of several kinds of tea sourced from different countries. The tea is brewed in a fine porcelain teapot that is embellished with the characteristic Friesian rose. It is then served in a manner that is rather unique: first a rock candy sugar, called *kluntjes*, is placed at the bottom of the cup, and this is used to sweeten multiple cups. The tea is topped with heavy cream and served without a spoon, as it is meant to be drunk unstirred, to be savoured in stages. Elsewhere, in Germany, despite the coffee habit, tea holds good ground and tea shops proliferate everywhere.

Drinking Tea in France

With the re-emergence of the popularity of the beverage, tea rooms or the Salon de Thé became a fashion by the late seventeenth century and they continue to be so. These usually have a delectable patisserie that is offered along with tea, served often in a beautifully furbished, elegant setting, complete with ornate mirrors and chandeliers. The long standing Mariage Freres Company that was founded in 1854 by two tea merchant brothers, Edouard and Henri Mariage, have highly rated tea salons in Paris, the French capital.

High Tea in England

The English tradition of afternoon tea was introduced sometime during the late eighteenth century by Anna, Duchess of Bedford. One summer day she experienced a 'sinking feeling' and inspired by the European style of tea service, invited friends to join her for an additional nibble at five o'clock in her rooms at Belvoir Castle.

Along with tea she served small cakes, sandwiches, (just around this time, the Earl of Sandwich had the idea of putting a filling between two slices of bread that would create one of the world's most popular snacks), and

assorted sweets. Other social hostesses took the cue, extending invitations for afternoon tea.

On the other hand, for the labourers and peasants, afternoon tea became high tea, a sort of main meal of the day, being a hybrid between lunch and dinner. It included a heavier menu with meats, mashed potatoes, peas, bread, cakes, and of course, tea. At work, employers began to allow 'tea breaks' as a mid-morning interlude for their workers. Tea became especially popular for its high sustenance value during the Industrial Revolution to help workers tide over long hours in factories.

Tea still remains one of the chief ambassadors of the English lifestyle. The ever popular tea shops in the country are a carry-over of the time when, in 1864, the woman manager of the Aerated Bread Company set the precedent of serving food and tea to her customers. Such tea shops are imbued with the charm of yesteryears, serving a classic cuisine that may include dainty sandwiches, shrimp or fish patés, and regional pastries like Scottish scones and English crumpets.

Typically, an afternoon tea service still carries gracious decorum. Try walking into the tea lounge at the heritage

Fortnum & Mason Store or the Ritz Hotel—or any well-appointed establishment that serves high tea in London in jeans and sneakers and you will be informed with cool politeness that a dress code is required.

Other Countries and Cultures

In the British Isles, the Irish surpass the English in their tea drinking, consuming four to six cups of tea, on an average, per day. They prefer a strong dark tea, usually taken with milk and sugar. During a traditional Irish wake, after a family member has passed away, it is common to have a pot on the boil throughout the night.

Tea gains even greater importance in the Middle East because alcohol is prohibited in these societies. In the Arab world, the beverage is had in little glasses, the size and shape of the glass varying across different regions. The Turks, for instance, drink strong black tea in tulip-shaped glasses, while Iraq and Jordan use decorated glasses in gold and crystal. The Egyptians, on the other hand, use glasses that are more regular and rounded. Their tea is a strong brew, served with plenty of sugar and no milk. In Morocco, it is the host not the hostess, who serves tea. It is common to see groups of men sitting in street cafés relaxing over Moroccan Mint tea, which is sweet green tea flavoured with mint, and taken in small glasses. A similar style of tea is taken all over North Africa, in countries like Algeria and Tunisia.

In Russia, tea holds almost as much importance as vodka. The drink became a rage when, in 1618, the Chinese ambassador presented Czar Alexis with a gift of several ornate chests of tea. The Russians first brew the tea concentrate in a small kettle. This is then poured into the cup and hot water is added. Sugar, lemon, honey or jam may be added to the tea. In some regions, a samovar supplies hot water for the tea all day long. Ornate tea glass holders as well as Lomonosov teaware embellished with a cobalt blue net design and 22-carat gold reflect the grandeur of the era of the Czars.

It is not always that tea is taken sweet. In high mountain cultures such as Tibet, Bhutan and Afghanistan, the brew is prepared by boiling the leaves for several hours and then churning it with yak butter and salt. The result is a pinkish purple tea that has a high caloric content to keep warm. Tea was introduced to Tibet via China sometime in the tenth century, and was popularised by the Sakya clan during the thirteenth century.

In Taiwan too, tea was first imported from Mainland China during the Ming and Ching dynasties. Tea culture here continues to flourish in the form of charming tea houses, with ceremonious tea presentations. Lately, the more contemporary Bubble Tea with its pearly tapioca balls floating in a tea base with fruit flavours or milk, has become a rage the world over. The Korean tea heritage also speaks of Buddhist monks who brought the drink from China during the Silla Dynasty, and the country has its own indigenous tea ceremony. South-east Asian countries like Singapore and Thailand also have a well-embedded tea culture. In Malaysia, tea takes the form of *Teh Tarik* or 'hand pulled' tea, being poured in quick movements from a height from one jug to another, creating a frothy cup.

Tea Trade and the Numbers Game

Over the years, the cultivation of tea spread to Latin American countries like Argentina and Brazil in the southern hemisphere. It also spread to other British colonies in Africa, and today, countries like Kenya, Malawi, Uganda, Tanzania and Zimbabwe grow and export tea. Turkey, in the Eurasian continent, ranks as one of the largest tea markets in the world, as, besides its high domestic consumption, it also cultivates tea along the Black Sea coast, much of which is exported. Moving east, countries like Nepal, Bangladesh, Indonesia, Vietnam and Taiwan all qualify in the order of world exports. Tea for export is also grown in Papua New Guinea in the Pacific Islands.

However, in the language of global tea economy, Kenya leads in tea exports. (430.41 million kg*) Next ranks China (321.79 million kg*) followed by Sri Lanka (304.49 million kg*) and India (201.08 million kg*). In the area of imports, the Russian Federation are the largest buyers, followed by the UK, Pakistan and the USA. As during its early beginnings, tea remains a significant component of international trade and continues to link the world commercially.

FACING PAGE Lemon with tea has always prevailed in western cultures, even while the practice of adding milk to tea was popularised in England.

OVERLEAF: A seemingly boundless expanse of tea gardens at Assam Company Limited's Greenwood Tea Estate.

ABOVE: Graded Orthodox teas as laid out in an office of a tea factory.

CHOICES
FOR THE
TEA LOVER

'The naming of teas is a difficult matter…
For starters each tea in this world belong
To the families Black or Green or Oolong;…
Then look more closely at these family trees—
Some include Indians along with Chinese.'

~ *T. S. Eliot*

In this age of consumer specialisation and soft drinks explosion, the world of tea continues to hold its place. And not surprisingly so, for there is an incredible range of teas that are being produced to present selections that go beyond quantification.

There are, for instance, a host of different hued selections that include black, green, oolong, yellow and white tea. Emerging trends are dictating the popularity of organic tea, together with new age interpretations like herbal teas, flavoured infusions and instant teas. There is a tea for every inclination.

Both Orthodox and CTC teas fall under the category of black tea. As they result from a higher degree of fermentation or oxidation, the finished product bears an appearance so dark that it is referred to as Black. In countries like China, Japan and Korea, such teas are often termed 'red', referring to their reddish-gold infusion.

Orthodox teas are an unfailing draw for a tea connoisseur, as their twisted long leaves are produced with a focus on top quality leaves and buds. Their special characters and selective attributes make them pricey, and even more expensive are teas that are hand rolled, or 'handmade'. An Orthodox tea may belong either from a particular region, or can be 'Single Estate' or being exclusive to a specific garden. Being generally light and delicate, such type of teas are best taken with a hint of milk, or even without milk.

RIGHT: Tea related gifts at Twinings Store, London.

CTC Teas

CTC teas marry well with milk, as they have a stronger body and a darker liquor. Being produced from a rapid mechanised process, the cells of the CTC leaf are torn down to cause greater oxidisation that gives these teas their strength. As their production output is quicker, they are more economical and are popular in the packaged market. In appearance and aroma, such teas are more generic, as the product would be a standardised result of adeptly blended teas from various gardens.

The type of black tea is recognised, among other factors, by its grading, which is mostly done under the terminology, 'Orange Pekoe' (pronounced as Peck-O). The word 'Orange' might sound incongruous for a 'black' tea, but it owes its name to the Dutch royal family, the House of Orange to whom these teas were first presented: while 'Pekoe' is a distortion of *Bai Hao*, the Chinese words for 'white tip' and refers to the young leaf bud that is covered with a fine white down, establishing the superior delicacy of the tea. 'Orange Pekoe' therefore gave implications of royal patronage and the tea was promoted to the Dutch public to suggest exclusivity.

This qualification of tea leaf grade with its rather poetic inflections, applies in particular to teas that come from India and Sri Lanka. It is not unusual to find a well-packaged tea in the market proclaiming a dreamy name of a faraway garden, with its label bearing a particular grading. It might be initialled with a 'Whole leaf' grading or a 'Broken leaf' grading, or the smaller 'Fannings' sizes and 'Dust' grades. The categories fall as under:

Whole Leaf Tea Grades

Flowery Orange Pekoe (FOP): This refers to high quality whole leaf tea made from the first two leaves and bud of the shoot.

Golden Flowery Orange Pekoe (GFOP): This is descriptive of the golden tips which are the delicate yellow tips at the end of the top bud.

Tippy Golden Flowery Orange Pekoe (TGFOP): This is FOP with a larger proportion of golden tips than GFOP. Another variation of this grade can be TGFOP1 or Tippy Golden Flowery Orange Pekoe Grade One.

Finest Tippy Golden Flowery Orange Pekoe (FTGFOP): This has an even greater quantity of tips than the FOP grade.

Supreme Finest Tippy Golden Flowery Orange Pekoe (SFTGFOP): This is very high quality FOP with an abundance of golden tips. In the case of Darjeeling teas, the 'S' indicates Supreme light coloured liquor.

Orange Pekoe (OP): This is a version of FOP, picked much later, and its rolling process is tighter.

Pekoe (P): This is larger in size, but does not have much golden tips.

Souchong (S): This is a twisted leaf picked from the bottom of the tea bush. China produces this grade which is used in their smoky teas.

FACING PAGE: Close-ups of Black tea grades; Orthodox and Green tea.
ABOVE: Graded Orthodox teas as laid out in an office of a tea factory. Orthodox teas have a long, twisted appearance.

Broken Leaf Tea Grades

Broken leaf grades follow very much the nomenclature of the whole leaf grades, with the addition of the initial 'B' to indicate 'Broken'. Hence there are grades like FBOP (Flowery Broken Orange Pekoe), GBOP (Golden Broken Orange Pekoe) and FGBOP (Flowery Golden Broken Orange Pekoe), TGFBOP (Tippy Golden Flowery Broken Orange Pekoe), Broken Orange Pekoe (BOP), BS (Broken Souchong) and BPS (Broken Pekoe Souchong) and so on.

Fannings and Dust

The smaller leaf particles fall into two categories, Fannings and Dust. While Fannings still have a recognisable coarse texture, Dust is just a fine powder made of tea particles left over after producing the higher grades of tea and is still of value, unlike the image its name conjures. Both these grades produce an even stronger and brighter liquor than CTC tea and are best taken with milk. In India the finest form of Dust is CD (Churamoni Dust), which is used for dhabha chai. It is so strong that it holds its flavour despite the constant boiling and substantial quantity of milk that goes into the preparation.

Grade also affects the brewing time. Wholeleaf teas usually need longer infusion times, whereas broken leaf teas require shorter steeping, and fannings and dust infuse the fastest.

Tea Bags

Tea bags command a never diminishing popularity as they are convenient and economical. The expense of manufacturing the tea bag is offset by the type of teas that are usually used in them, mostly Fannings, Dust or CTC. Such type of teas do not expand much when steeped, so they are suited for the confines of the bag and infuse quickly to create a brew. A few dips do the job. Orthodox tea bags are not as common, being rather a niche speciality and are therefore higher priced. These are usually pyramid-shaped so that the design allows greater space for the long leaves to expand when dipped in hot water.

Green Tea

Green tea has always been the prerogative of the East, in countries like China, Japan, Korea and Taiwan. Such teas are produced after a minimum process of fermentation, that result in very little oxidation, and the green colour of the leaf is retained. A quick application of heat is applied to the leaves, either by steam or by pan frying, after which they are rolled and dried.

When prepared, they have a pale greenish yellow colour, and they are never taken with milk. Some of the world's finest green tea comes from China. Teas like Dragon Well from Hangzhou in Zhejiang Province and Silver Needle from Hunan Province vie with several more

well-known exotic names such as Rain Flower, White Cloud, Jade Sword, Dragon Pearl, etc. Gunpowder Tea is another type of green tea that has each leaf rolled into a small round pellet.

Japanese green tea also has a traditional claim to fame. The idyllic tea region of Shizuoka Prefecture west of Tokyo has undulating hills with closely-contoured tea bushes. Here grows the major produce of Japan's green tea varieties, including Bancha, Sencha and Hojicha.

Among the most prized is the delicate Gyokuro or 'Precious Dew' whose bushes are covered with bamboo mats so that the tea grows in semi-darkness, and a higher chlorophyll content is induced. This results in the vivid green colour of Maccha powdered tea.

On the northern-most point of Shizuoka lies the revered Mt Fuji, the region from where comes the O-cha variety. Some of the best teas come from Uji in Kyoto, as well as from Yame in Fukuoka Prefecture.

In the rest of the world, the trend for green tea is on the increase. In India, for instance, it is being produced in all the tea regions.

Assam green teas have a stronger, almost nutty, flavour, and are different from those of China and Japan.

Some of the finest green tea comes from Darjeeling with flavours that are sharper and more delicate, arising as they do, from the Chinese stock. Kangra Valley green teas have a good market in Afghanistan and the Middle East. Nilgiri green teas resemble those from nearby Sri Lanka.

FACING PAGE LEFT AND RIGHT: Pyramid-shaped tea bags are used for the Orthodox leaf. Green tea leaf is lesser oxidised than black tea and hence the light colour of its brew.

ABOVE: Shizuoka Prefecture in the mountain region of Mt Fuji produces some of Japan's finest green teas.

Oolong Tea

These teas lie between black and green teas as they are semi-fermented. Also originating from China, they get their English name from the Chinese characters *Wu* 'black' and *Lung*, 'dragon'.

In this case, the fermentation time for the leaf is variable, during which oxidation is controlled, depending on the type of tea being made. For light oolong teas, the amount of oxidation can be anywhere from five to forty per cent while in darker oolong teas it is sixty to seventy per cent, as compared to black teas where there is hundred per cent oxidation. The tea is then fired, traditionally in hot woks. As a result, different aromas can emerge from these teas. They can be sweetish and fruity, or woody and roasted with a heavy aroma, or with fresh green aromas, all depending on the style of production.

The Wuyi mountains in China's Fujian province are famous for Tie Guan Yin or 'monkey-picked tea'. It is said that in the early eighteenth century, the monks grew tea here, and as this remote and high region was difficult to access, they trained monkeys to pick the leaves. The name of the tea means 'Iron Goddess' or 'Iron Bodhisattva', as it has dark iron-coloured leaves that yield a tea that is delicate and almost ethereal in flavour.

Oolongs from Taiwan are also reputed, with some popular names like Dong Ding, Frozen Summit or Ice Peak. Other countries that produce such teas are Vietnam, Indonesia, Kenya and Malawi. In India too, oolong teas are prepared by several gardens. Makaibari and Goomtee Tea Estates of the Darjeeling region, for example, produce some good oolongs that have a fresh palate.

White Tea

This type of tea is limited and rare. It is derived from a picking of young buds even before they begin to unfurl. Covered as they are, with fine white downy hairs, the tea liquor is so pale that it is almost white. The buds are sundried and the tender leaves are processed with great care and to a bare minimum to prevent fermentation, so that the fresh taste of the tea is maintained. Only the most passionate tea lovers can be willing to pay the exorbitant price for their incomparable delicacy of taste. While green teas may have a slightly raw taste, white teas are described as light and floral.

Some examples are Bai Hao Yinzhen or Silver Needle and Bai Mudan or White Peony, that come from China's Fujian Province. Despite China's edge, Makaibari White tea from India was given recognition by being used at the 2008 Beijing Olympics. These types of teas are also produced in all the tea regions of India.

Yellow Tea

Such teas result from a process similar to green tea, but with a slower drying phase, so the damp leaves are allowed to sit until they turn yellow. They are oxidised even lesser than the oolongs, usually being fired in a wok, and then baked over slow heat resulting in a yellowish appearance. They develop a clear light taste, as opposed to the vegetal taste of green tea. Junshan Yinzhen or Silver Needle Yellow from Hunan Province, Meng Ding Huangya from Sichuan Province, and Huang Tang or Yellow Broth from Zhejiang Province, are some of the recognised yellow teas from China.

Pu-erh Tea

Pu-erh is post-fermented tea that is usually available as a compressed brick, but sometimes it can also be in loose form. It is usually made from unoxidised green tea processed from a large leaf variety from the Yunnan Province. It is then 'ripened' or aged so that it gives a dark liquor.

FACING PAGE : A compressed tea 'cake' of Pu-erh tea from China.
ABOVE: White tea is rare and expensive.
BELOW: Oolong teas are semi-fermented and lie between black and green teas.

SPECIALITY TEAS

THE MADHATTER'S TEA PARTY

Anhui Green Tea

£65.00 per 100g

Welcome to Harrods

Organic Tea

An increasing awareness of the hazards of pollutants and chemical pesticides has led to a rising demand for organic teas that are grown completely in the natural way. Fertilisers take the form of compost, neem cake and castor cake and specially prepared herbicides are employed for the nurture and care of the tea bushes.

While Indian teas from Kangra have been traditionally organic, several gardens across other tea regions are also adopting methods for organic tea cultivation.

In Assam, Rossell Tea's Dikom Tea Estate produces fine organic Orthodox teas in a well monitored environment where four types of shade trees have been planted so that they shed leaves in different cycles to maintain the ecological balance. In this region too, Chamong Tee's Maud Tea Estate prepare their own fertiliser, using cowdung layered with wheat chaff that is cured and cut into cubes.

At Darjeeling's Makaibari Tea Estate, Swaraj Banerjee, with his driving commitment to enforce bio-organic practices, has heavy afforestation around his tea gardens. Virgin rain forests give way to tiers of leguminous trees, descending to mulch banks of grasses and fruit trees, amongst which nestle the tea bushes, protected by a plethora of ground vegetation. 'The layered plantings provide a natural compost and release nitrogen, which is an important requirement for the tea bushes. Organic tea cultivation is a matter of living in rhythm with nature…' says Banerjee.

In South India, at Korakundah Tea Estate, earthworm vermi-culture is employed to make fertiliser. Gardens such as these need to adhere to specified parameters to qualify for an organic certification. The flavours and aromas of the tea that they produce remain much the same as in non-organic cultivation, but they are priced higher as their growth is slow and their yield per acre lower. However, such teas herald a welcome awakening to conserving the fragility of the earth's environment.

PREVIOUS PAGE: Harrods Department Store in London has a discerning selection of tea. It also offers an elegant afternoon tea service in its restaurant. Harrods had its beginnings as a small grocery shop in Brompton Road that was set up by Charles Henry Harrod in 1849, who always highlighted tea as a part of his merchandise. By 1902, its repute had grown to draw patronage from eminent personalities as well as members of the British Royal Family.

ABOVE: Packaged brands from various countries provide infinite choices for the lover of tea.

FACING PAGE: The Delhi-based 'Aap Ki Pasand' tea company markets *masala* chai under its brand 'San-cha'.

Blended & Flavoured Teas

These teas are a predictable product of taste, and go by brand names that have their own following. Teas like English Breakfast, Irish Breakfast and Scottish Breakfast are blends of robust black teas that have body and strength of flavour so that they can be taken with milk.

Being of high caffeine content, they give a good kick-off to the day. Afternoon blends are usually a mix of lighter teas, and can be taken on their own without milk. Russian Caravan, a well-known blend, may, among others, even contain some oolong varieties. Each tea company will have its own special formula for creating its own blends.

In India, Sanjay Kapur, at the flagship store of his tea Company, Aap Ki Pasand, Delhi, says: 'We exploit the complex and exciting characters of regional teas that are available from the immensely varying *terroir* of this country to create blends for every palate.'

Being a well-honed tea taster, he has developed numerous interesting varieties to market them under his own brand name San-Cha. These are available at international duty-free shops across India, and are exported, particularly to the Far East. His formula for Indian *masala* Chai scores well with his customers. It is a combination of discerningly sourced black teas mixed with authentic spices so that the tea releases a genuine, wholesome flavour.

Several other varieties of blends can be created in this manner by combining herbs, flowers and spices, the aromas of which are picked up by the tea leaves as their cell structure is hygroscopic. The technique of flavouring goes back to the days of Chinese tea discovery; when tea growers planted peaches, plums, apricots and sweet smelling flowering bushes to provide shade and moisture to their teas, they realised that these flavours had pleasing influences on tea. They have continued to be masters of this art. Their widely popular Jasmine Tea has freshly cut flowers that are added to the tea leaves during the oxidation process. Lapsong Souchong is made by drying black tea over smoking pine needles. Lotus Tea from Vietnam is made by stuffing green tea leaves into the blossom of a particular type of lotus and allowing it to absorb the fragrance.

Finally, in its simplest aspect, there is always the option of making an amateur blend at home, by combining different types of tea leaves to be brewed in the pot. In this way, aspects of colour, flavour and aroma can be adjusted according to preference.

Scented Teas

The cell structure of the tea leaf is capable of picking up surrounding aromas. In this sense, it works in favour of creating tea blends that can be combined with sweet-scented components like flowers, herbs and fruits. Innumerable flavours of tea can be imaginatively created by simply scenting the leaves with various extracts like rose, vanilla, chrysanthemum and many more. Jasmine tea pearls never cease to fascinate, wherein scented tea leaves are rolled and woven into a pearl-like shape that unfurls in the cup.

By far, the most well known of scented teas is Earl Grey. This is a combination of blended black tea from China or Darjeeling scented with oil from the peel of bergamot, a Canton orange.

Be it green or black, countless versions of scented teas can be produced.While a purist tea drinker may not really enjoy flavoured teas, they definitely synchronise with the changing profile of tea drinkers. The story goes the Earl Grey, the Georgian prime minister was given cases of this tea by a Chinese Mandarin. He liked it so much that he brought it home to England and asked Twinings to recreate it for him.

Twinings then became the first company to create the original Earl Grey. Charles Grey became the British Prime Minister around 1830, and would have been instrumental in ending the monopoly on tea imports which had become so profitable for the East India Company. Over the ages, the popularity of this tea has never diminished, and it is being produced by several well-known companies including Lipton.

Herbal Tea & Tisanes

Although they are called 'tea', herbal infusions are simply a 'tisane', and do not have tea leaves at all. Rooibos is a well-known herbal red tea from South Africa, derived from a particular variety of bush. Flowers and plant materials such as camomile, lemon grass, and liquorice root are dried and sold commercially either loose or in tea bags and when steeped they release a flavourful infusion. In itself, a herbal tea may be prepared by giving a long boil to strong flavoured natural components like anise and caraway, with or without the tea leaves. Some of these herbs are valued for their medicinal properties and such preparations date back to ancient China and Egypt. Infusions of various herbs such as *'tulsi'* have always been used in ancient India's medicinal Ayurveda.

Instant Tea

This is a convenience product in a freeze dried form in which all solubles have been extracted by a mechanised process, leaving only 2.5 per cent of the water aspect in the powder. Both hot and cold tea instant mixes are available, the packaging only states the amount of water to be added as per the quantity of powder. Companies like the Swiss multi-national Nestle are market leaders in instant teas, making them available in fruity flavours such as lemon or peach. Chilled bottled green and oolong teas derived from instant tea powders are also refreshing and widely consumed. Contemporary technology has added several new dimensions to tea, so that it can be enjoyed by all, in any form, anytime, anywhere. A tribute as it were, to the refreshing and calming qualities of this beverage.

FACING PAGE: Jasmine tea has pellets rolled like pearls.
ABOVE: [CLOCKWISE FROM TOP LEFT]
Herbal teas can be of medicinal value; Camomile tea cures insomnia;
Blends often carry exotic names to express exclusivity of flavour;
A fragrant blend of Assam black tea combined with dried rose petals.

Choices for the Tea Lover 261

ABOVE: A tea shop in Hamburg exhibits a variety of Darjeeling Tea from India.

FACING PAGE: Tea leaves and brew set out on display.

A CUPFUL OF HEALTH

'My experience…convinced me that tea was better than brandy, and during the last six months in Africa I took no brandy, even when sick, taking tea instead.'

~ Theodore Roosevelt

Tea deserves all the preference it receives from those who relish it. The beverage not only has a high sustenance value, but has also been proven to endow several positive effects on health. In a world of progressive scientific research, the biological composition of the tea plant has come under study because of the correlation of longevity and health in many ancient tea drinking cultures like China and Japan.

In its everyday aspect, tea is considered a beneficial agent for relieving fatigue and aiding clarity of thought, besides being favourable for digestion. Although its stimulating effects are derived from its caffeine content, unlike coffee, drinking tea in large quantities does not cause hyperactivity, insomnia, or stomach irritation, as this compound is present in a ratio that is half the level of caffeine in coffee. A 190 ml cup of tea contains approximately 40–50 mg of caffeine, while full flavour coffees average 110–120 mg per cup.

Green, oolong, white and pu-erh tea infusions contain even less caffeine than black teas. Not only do they undergo lesser oxidation, but it is so because such teas are made with multiple infusions: since water is added more than once, and as the liquor gets poured off, it reduces the content of caffeine. Caffeine is considered safe when it is consumed at a dose of 400 mg or less per day which would include the intake of soft drinks such as colas. Hence, be it black or green tea, whichever it may be, it is safer to enjoy several cups of tea rather than multiple cups of coffee.

An Invaluable Antioxidant

In all, this exhilarating beverage ranks as a useful component of nature's health repository. The leaves of the Camellia Sinensis, especially the buds and tender shoots contain catechins and polyphenols. These are part of the molecular family of flavonoids that are beneficiary compounds made by plants.

Tea gains much of its refreshing pungency from its secondary ingredient, polyphenols TF and TR which are derived from a precursor magic compound Epi-gallo-catechin-gallate (EGCG) that is found in green tea leaves.

Its content is a little higher in green tea, as compared to the fully fermented black teas, because during the oxidation process, most of the catechins are converted into complex polyphenols, thearubigins and theaflavins. Oolong tea contains a mix of catechins and polyphenols, as it is semi-fermented. Instant and iced teas, on the other hand, do not have the same amount of polyphenols as an equal volume of brewed tea. Instant teas are generally derived from low grade source material.

All these different types of catechins and polyphenols have great value as they serve as antioxidants that neutralise the damage caused by an excess of free radicals in the body. The latter, in simple terms, are the by-product of the normal process by which oxygen is combined with glucose in our body cells, to make energy; they are not in themselves harmful. In fact, the immune system may itself produce free radicals to neutralise viruses and bacteria. It is only when they are produced in excess that they begin to attack the cell membranes and tissues and pave the way for cancer, besides perpetuating blockage that plays a role in heart disease and accelerates the ageing process.

Antioxidants act as vital scavengers that mop up the damage caused by rogue free radicals by neutralising them and consequently preventing cell and tissue damage.

Although antioxidants in the form of catechins and flavonoids are found to some extent in red wine and in green leafy vegetables like broccoli and spinach, and fruits such as apples and berries as well as in dark chocolate, tea remains one of the most important sources of antioxidants.

A study at the Antioxidant Research Centre in London published in *Free Radical Research* in February 1999, put forth the following formula:

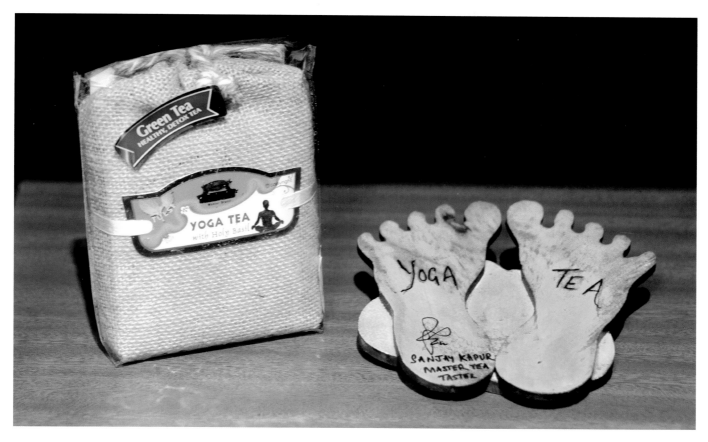

2 cups of black tea=1 glass of red wine=7 glasses of orange juice=20 glasses of apple juice.

Tea, therefore, with its high content of antioxidants, is a potential agent for fighting cancer. Similarly, biological research also reveals that the antioxidants in tea can counter the artery-damaging potential of the reactive free radicals. According to TNO, a Dutch innovation organisation, quercetin, a valuable polyphenol found in tea and other vegetables and fruits, has anti-oxidative properties and prevents the formation of plaque.

In this manner, it helps the endothelial layers of the arteries to remain flexible for good circulation and makes the blood cells less prone to clotting and is a good preventive for heart disease and strokes. Although these diseases are attributed in great part to genetic and lifestyle factors, health studies do show some positive insights into the antioxidant benefits of this beverage.

Moreover, the catechins in tea offer the advantage of being an aid for killing infection as they block viruses and bacteria from hooking on to cell walls. Therefore they can help protect against diseases like influenza, food poisoning, dysentery and cholera. By the same measure, they can kill mouth bacteria that are harmful for teeth and gums and lead to periodontal disease.

Tea also improves the functioning of the intestines by blocking the growth of bad bacteria and enhancing good bacteria and is therefore a good digestive. It is said to be detoxifying as the catechins can scavenge harmful heavy metals like lead, chromium, mercury, which may get ingested with food.

FACING PAGE: A blend of green tea with basil marketed as a symbol of healthy calm.

ABOVE: A tea box with a presentation of packaged blends that create their own individual flavours.

Tea for Beauty & Relaxation

In itself tea has no calories at all, and it is merely the addition of sugar in each cup of tea that leads to weight gain. Milk however, is not objectionable, as long as it is just a dash.

There is also the belief that green tea helps in slimming. While it can by no means be construed as a miracle drink, green tea is known to give a metabolic boost that may shed off a few extra calories by about four per cent. By virtue of its antioxidant qualities that help fight ageing and skin damage, tea extracts with their refreshing aromas are also used in facial creams, skin packs and perfumes.

The comforting qualities of the beverage are no old wives tale either. There is a natural bioflavonoid found in tea that has been found to significantly increase endorphin levels, which in turn reduce pain and anxiety so that in cases of shock and stress, a cup of tea soothes the nerves.

Tea as a Source of Minerals

The tea plant has the natural ability to absorb fluoride from the soil and so a tea infusion readily releases this mineral into the water, making it a beneficial drink for healthy teeth. It is estimated that a single cup provides 0.1 mg of fluoride and can provide forty-five per cent of the body's daily requirement. Studies have also shown that there are some estrogenic compounds in tea, together with elements of manganese that help in increasing bone mass by five per cent, thereby reducing fracture risk. It also contains potassium, a mineral vital for maintaining body fluid levels. The beverage acts as a diuretic. This benign brew is also known to have Vitamin C, zinc and folic acid, and is therefore regularly recommended for pregnant women.

Finally, it is not to be forgotten that during the days of its discovery in China, the beverage was recognised at first for its remedial worth. Modern health research still continues to reiterate this fact.

FACING PAGE: End of a spa session at The Imperial, New Delhi; a guest reclines and reaches out to sip green tea.

ABOVE AND BELOW: A yoga master strikes a posture for meditation; she will end her regimen with some green tea.

OVERLEAF: Aap ki Pasand tea parlour, New Delhi.

A Cupful of Health 267

RECIPES WITH TEA

'The very act of preparing and serving tea encourages conversation. The little spaces in time created by teatime rituals call out to be filled with conversation. Even the tea itself—warm and comforting—inspires a feeling of relaxation and trust that fosters shared confidences.'

~ *Emilie Barnes*

Besides the archetypical tea preparations, including the ever-popular masala chai that has an established repute across India, and has presently transcended international borders with ever-increasing global demand, nowadays tea bars and luxury hotels within India are blazing new trends by developing innovative tea recipes, taking benefit of the generous and accommodating disposition of the leaf. Tea readily absorbs flavours from other additives, even as the brew lends itself to interesting adaptations, given its many aromas. Together with the rich hues of its amber-coppery liquor, the beverage can result in the creation of attractive and exotic thirst quenching refreshments, and it also partners well in the making of some heady cocktails. And what's more: the innovative epicurean can go a step further and combine these very attributes for creating a special twist to food preparation, so that tea can also prove to be a delight for the taste buds.

The classic Indian recipe, of water, milk and tea leaves combined, still holds good. Sometimes this is combined with *tulsi patta*, the Indian basil leaf, besides other additives that are considered curative. Indian home-grown recipes can never diminish in popularity. While nowadays tea can be trendy, the classic Indian recipe, blended with natural ingredients like lemon, ginger or cinnamon, continues to provide significant health benefits.

FACING PAGE AND RIGHT: A delicate tea service the western way.

Truly and Purely Indian

Masala Chai
Serves 4

Infused with the flavour of spices, this tea is best had with a generous helping of milk and sugar. Well loved by all, especially during the cold winter months, or simply as a pick-me-up.

INGREDIENTS

Water		3 cups
Milk	full cream	1½ cup
Cinnamon	stick, 1 inch piece	1 no
Cardamom	green, lightly crushed	4 nos
Cloves		2 nos
Sugar	6tsp (or as required)	
Tea leaves	black /CTC	3 tsp

METHOD: Heat the water in a saucepan and bring it to a boil. Put in the spices and sugar, allow boiling for two minutes. Add tea leaves, bring it to a boil again and brew for about one minute. Next, add milk, bringing it to a boil once more, and simmer for another thirty seconds. Pour the tea into cups/glasses and serve.

Kashmiri Kahwa
Serves 4

Evocative of the unmatched valley of Kashmir.

INGREDIENTS

Water	4½ cups
Cinnamon stick, 1 inch piece	1 no
Cardamom green, lightly crushed	4 nos
Sugar	40 gms/to taste
Tea leaves green	1 heaped tsp
Saffron strands	1 pinch
Almonds blanched, peeled, chopped	4 nos

METHOD: Heat the water in a saucepan and bring it to a boil. Put in the spices and sugar, allow boiling for two-three minutes. Add tea leaves and saffron, remove from flame, cover with a lid and allow brewing for about five minutes. Put one chopped almond in each cup/bowl. Pour the tea over the almonds and serve hot.

Grandma's Chai for Cough and Cold
Serves 1

Ginger and spices act well in tea to alleviate those nagging symptoms.

INGREDIENTS

Water	¾ cup
Milk	½ cup
Cardamom	1 pod
Fresh ginger (mulched)	2 pea sized pieces
Whole black pepper	1-2 big size
Cinnamon stick	1/8" to 1/6"
Black tea leaves	1 tsp

METHOD: On a hard surface, crush all the spices together and put them in the saucepan. Simmer for a couple of minutes for the flavours to infuse, and then add the tea leaves, water and milk. Keep on a low fire, on the boil for five to ten minutes, stirring now and then. Add sugar to taste. Strain and serve. The idea is to evaporate the water from the tea, while mixing in the spices into the leftover tea. You may have to experiment with the quantity of water and milk to the final quantity of tea. For example, if it is a 2:1 ratio, (2 cups of milk plus water for making 1 cup of chai), one cup of water is boiled off in the process. This brings out the smooth taste of the chai.

ABOVE: 'Chai' in Gurmukhi, the Punjabi script. Punjab is a region where masala chai is popular, usually taken in a mug or glass.

Tea Innovations from
The Imperial*, New Delhi

Harking back to the era of colonialism in India, The Imperial is one of the first hotels in Delhi that came into being. It was intrinsic to Edwin Lutyens' master design that was made when the decision was taken to shift the capital from Calcutta to Delhi, during the Coronation Durbar of King George V in 1911. Built in the 1930s by Late Sardar Bahadur Ranjit Singh, it became a venue for several illustrious personalities like Mahatma Gandhi, Jawaharlal Nehru and Mohammad Ali Jinnah to meet and hold discussions at the time when the early stirrings for Independence had mobilised into voices of determination. It is said that together, they conferred with Lord Mountbatten, the last Viceroy of India, to discuss the transition to freedom and the creation of Pakistan. Considering the English penchant for the beverage that had, by now, percolated into India, these discussions would have probably been held over several cups of tea.

Today the Period grandeur of the past can still be enjoyed over a tea service at the hotel's Atrium Tea Lounge where its ambience, complete with a sumptuous classic tea menu scripts some of the drama of the Victorian age.

And yet, as being a part of its metamorphosis into the contemporary, The Imperial offers our readers recipes that go beyond convention, being based on the fusion of tea flavours with imaginative improvisation. Clearly, tea can be enjoyed in any form.

*Member of Preferred Hotels & Resorts Worldwide

ABOVE: The Atrium Tea Lounge at The Imperial is set in a high domed space with Victorian pillars, paned doors and a gracious central fountain. Its menu has some of the choicest Single Estate teas, as well as selections of Assam, Organic, Earl Grey and Makaibari.

Refreshing Coolers

Lemon Ice Tea
Serves 1

The tanginess of lemon and the astringency of tea combine well to create this classic cooler.

INGREDIENTS

Brewed tea

Sweet-and-sour-lemon mix to taste

METHOD: Fill a high ball glass with ice cubes. Add some sweet and sour mix and top up with tea brew. Garnish with lemon slices.

Blood Orange Ice Tea
Serves 1

The colours orange and red combine with tea to present this cool beauty.

INGREDIENTS:

Brewed tea	
Orange juice	60 ml
Grenadine syrup	a dash
Sweet-and-sour-lemon mix to taste	

METHOD: Fill a highball glass with ice cubes. Add the grenadine syrup and sweet and sour mix. Top up with tea brew and orange juice. Garnish with orange slices.

Citrus Delight
Serves 1

The tea base in this cooler goes well with the zesty flavours of pineapple and orange.

INGREDIENTS

Brewed tea	
Orange juice	60 ml
Pineapple juice	60 ml
Sweet-and-sour-lemon mix to taste	

METHOD: Add all the ingredients together and serve in a high ball glass filled with ice cubes. Garnish with orange slices.

Celebrating Tea at the Bar

Hot Toddy
Serves 1

Cognac assumes a new garb and is curative too—thanks to tea!

INGREDIENTS

Cognac	60 ml
Honey	30 ml
Cardamom	3-4 pcs
Cinnamon, clove, ginger	a few pieces
Black pepper	to taste
Lemon juice	15 ml
Brewed hot Assam tea	

METHOD: Crush all the spices and boil them in the tea brew. Place some pieces of ginger and spices at the bottom of a balloon brandy glass. Pour the spiced brew and add the honey. Lastly add a shot of cognac.

Voodoo
Serves 1

Blue Curacao and white rum partner with the boldness of Assam tea to create magic.

INGREDIENTS

White Rum	30 ml
Blue Curacao liqueur	30 ml
Sweet-and-sour-lemon mix	a dash
Brewed Assam tea.	

METHOD: Take a highball glass and fill it with ice. Pour the rum and blue Curacao. Add a dash of sweet and sour mix. Lastly top up with the tea brew, so that the dark colour of Assam tea sits atop the alcohol mix. Serve chilled.

Spirited Punch
Serves 1

With a tea base of the exclusive orange bergamot flavours of Earl Grey tea, this drink, created from a combination of five ingredients, enhances the party spirit.

INGREDIENTS:

Scotch Whiskey	45 ml
Peach juice	100 ml
Lemon juice	10 ml
Honey	30 ml or to taste
Lemon grass stick	20 gm

METHOD: Give a good shake to all the ingredients so that they mix well together. Pour them into a highball glass and top up with sparkling water. Serve chilled, garnished with lemon grass.

OVERLEAF: [CLOCKWISE FROM TOP LEFT]
Citrus Delight; Tea Poached Egg with Noodles; Hot Toddy; Voodoo, The Magical Touch; Tea Jelly with Caviar; Spirited Punch.

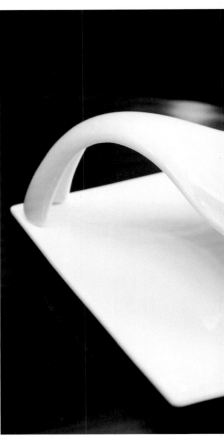

Tea for the Gourmet

Rosehip Tea Consommé with Star Anise, topped with Mint Foam
Serves 1

A light and healthy start with the beneficial qualities of rosehip tea, even as its delicate flavours harmonise with other ingredients, so gentle on digestion. Green tea with dried rose petals may be used as substitute.

INGREDIENTS

Rosehip tea	10 gms
Star anise	1 no
Orange segments	5 nos
Pineapple cubes	4 nos
Hot milk	75 ml
Fresh mint	3 sprigs
Dried mint powder	2 gms
Sugar	20 gms
Hot water	100 ml
Satay stick	1 no

METHOD: In hot water add rosehip tea, fresh mint, star anise, some orange segments and fresh mint leaves and keep aside till it reaches room temperature (may be around 15min).Slowly strain the mixture and transfer to a serving tumbler. Now to the hot milk add mint powder and whisk till it forms a froth. Sprinkle some sugar on the rest of the orange segments and on the diced pineapple. Caramelise these with blow torch or in a pan and string them on a satay stick. Gently take the mint froth and pour it on top of the rosehip tea. Serve the consommé at room temperature, garnished with the prepared satay stick.

Green Tea Marinated Tofu in Watermelon, Ginger and Pock Choy
Serves 1

This mild appetiser is laced with the delicacy of green tea flavours that are subtle and unobtrusive so that they complement the accompanying ingredients.

INGREDIENTS

Green tea	10 gms
Tofu	60 gms
Water melon hearts	60 gms
Ginger julienne	2 gms
Tri colour pepper juliennes	3 gms each
Leek juliennes	2 gms
Pock choy leaves	25 gms
Sweet soya sauce	5 ml
Refined oil	few drops
Chopped coriander	3 sprigs

METHOD: Make a green tea with the leaves and leave cut roundels of tofu to rest in the infusion for at least fifteen minutes. Heat oil in a pan and toss the rest of the ingredients in it, except the watermelon. Arrange thinly sliced water melon pieces on a plate and top them up with the tossed mixture. Lastly, arrange the green tea marinated tofu on top. Add the soya sauce and garnish with chopped coriander. Serve warm.

Black Tea Poached Egg with Cha Soba Noodles and Soya
Serves 1

Earl Grey tea imparts its special aroma to the poached egg and in combination with green tea soba noodles it makes a relished breakfast dish or even a main meal.

INGREDIENTS

Earl Grey tea	15 gms
Egg	1 no
Cha soba noodles	50 gms
Chopped coriander	15 gms
Chives	3 gms
Brown onion juliennes	3 gms
Japanese pickled ginger juliennes	4 gms
Chopped spring onion	5 gms
Seaweed juliennes	2 gms
Sesame seeds	2 mg
Water	100 ml

METHOD: Boil water with Earl Grey tea and coriander and simmer for a few minutes. Break the egg in a bowl and gently place it in the simmering tea liquid. Meanwhile blanch the cha soba noodles and keep them aside. Once the egg is poached to medium, gently transfer it to a serving plate. Now roll the cooked cha soba noodles and pile them on top of the poached egg. Garnish with the rest of the ingredients. Sprinkle sesame seeds and serve warm.

Chai Masala Sorbet
Serves 1

A cool French-style iced dessert created with an imaginative fusion taste of Indian masala chai.

INGREDIENTS

Masala Tea	45 ml
Water	100 ml
Sugar	15 gms
Liquid Glucose	5 gms
Stabiliser	8 gms

METHOD: Mix all the ingredients and bring to boil. Remove and rest the mixture until it cools down to room temperature. Pour it in an ice cream machine and churn for about twenty minutes. Remove and de-freeze it for thirty minutes. Serve frozen.

Darjeeling Tea and Evaporated Milk Jelly with Strawberry Caviar
Serves 1

The delicate flavours of Darjeeling tea come through in this specially prepared jelly dessert, complete with a fruity caviar that highlights the dish.

INGREDIENTS

Darjeeling tea	5 gms
Evaporated milk	60 gms
Sugar	45 gms
Gelatine leaf	1 no
Water	60 ml

FOR THE STRAWBERRY CAVIAR

Strawberry juice	30 ml
Agar-Agar	3 gms
Chilled oil	100 ml

METHOD: Boil the water and add the Darjeeling tea leaves to it. Boil evaporated milk with sugar and gelatine. Mix half of the tea mixture to the evaporated milk. Bring down to room temperature and pour it in a martini glass and refrigerate. Add the rest of the tea mixture in a saucepan and cook to reduce it. Serve with Strawberry Caviar on top.

FOR THE STRAWBERRY CAVIAR
Heat the strawberry juice with agar-agar and keep aside, stirring continuously. Now start putting drop by drop of the mixture to the chilled oil. The drops of the mixture turn into small fine balls as they touch the oil. Strain the balls and wash them with chilled water. Drain the water and serve the strawberry caviar with the dessert.

Green Tea Crème Brulee

Serves 1

Green tea flavours add a new twist to this classic French dessert.

INGREDIENTS

Green tea	4 gms
Cream Elle & Vire (double whipping cream)	100 gms
Sugar	15 gms
Egg yolk (approximately 3 eggs)	40 gms

METHOD: Cook the cream with green tea in a saucepan until it boils. Remove from the fire and add sugar and egg yolk separately to the cream. Cook the mixture once more in a double boiler until it thickens. Strain. Pour it in the mould and set in a refrigerator for an hour. Sprinkle sugar on top of the Crème Brulee and torch it until the sugar caramalises and forms a crisp crust. Alternatively, you can heat the back of a metal spoon until it is red hot and run it over the sugar in brisk movements to achieve the same effect.

FINALLY THE PERFECT CUP OF TEA

The perfect cup of tea cannot be a definitive recipe, as its 'perfection' is relative and hinges on individual choice. Almost every tea drinker prefers his own liking of brand, strength, preference of the amount of additives like milk and sugar—or no additives at all. The romance with tea is a very personal relationship.

However, the traditional method of getting the best results from your tea, as recommended by tea connoisseurs, is as follows:

Use, of course, your favourite quality tea leaf or tea bags that have been well stored in an airtight jar. Remember, that the moisture content in the end product of good, freshly packed tea is only 2.5%–3% and ideally, should be maintained as far as possible, once the packaging is opened.

Swirl a little boiling water around in the teapot before using it. In this way, the pot gets warmed so that the water, when poured in it for steeping does not cool down too quickly. Empty the hot water and place one tea bag (6 floz) or 1 level teaspoon (2–3 gm) for each cup.

Make sure that the water used is fresh and not over boiled. It should be just off a rolling boil.

Cover the teapot with a quilted tea cosy, so that it contains the heat, and allow the tea to steep for three to five minutes (this will depend on the type of brand and quality, and will be determined by your own judgement based on trial and error).

If you are using tea bags, remove them after the steeping period, without squeezing them. (Squeezing can press out some of the bitter polyphenols that remain in the leaf.)

Pour hot tea from the pot into the cups and enjoy it with whatever additives you like. While some people like to take their tea by adding a dash of milk, there is a school of tea-drinkers who believe in 'MIF' or milk-in-first— just a right amount—as it prevents degradation of the tea brew when it is poured in afterwards. Then there are others who like to add a hint of lemon that mingles with the tea aroma. And there are those who profess that tea is best enjoyed simply on its own, without either milk or lemon. Adding sugar or saccharine products, are, of course, a matter of taste. Start drinking the tea while it is still too hot to take a full gulp. The feel of the scalding hot tea making its way down your throat through small sips is what the whole experience is about. You can take bigger mouthfuls later into the cup.

ABOVE: A finely contoured cup from the German pottery studio, Rosenthal, highlights the delicacy of tea, supported by figurines from the same company. Tea drinking has led to the development of several historic porcelain brands that moved on to include art forms as well.

Rajan's
Vision

My Journey as a photographer became an integral part of my life and continues to be so. It has brought in joy and happiness; given me immense satisfaction to channel my inherent talent. Working on Chai: The Experience of Indian Tea gave me the opportunity to shoot my favourite subjects—people, landscapes and a bit of wild life.

As a young boy, my love for nature and outdoor activities was endless. Art in many forms—creating models, singing, drawing or painting—came naturally to me.

In my drawings and paintings, besides the subject itself, it was the frame in which the work sat that aroused my interest. This innate fascination connected me in a very natural way to photography.

I admired the work of Henri Cartier Bresson, who shot 'off the cuff', so to say, but who, in the true sense, was a master of composition.

With the purchase of my first SLR in 1990 my journey as a photographer took its first steps, together with my visit to the first B&W Photo-Exhibition of S. Paul, who in time became my guru and companion. We shared long journeys to far off destinations. And I learnt a lot about practical photography.

During this period I visited Pushkar, a mystical, near-magical place in Rajasthan, India. The annual Pushkar Fair is one of the most photographed events in the world.

Whilst here, spurred on by the curiosity of a beginner as well as the charm of Pushkar, I managed to take exclusive aerial shots, and had a narrow escape when the balloon fell from the sky! Pushkar, for me, is one very memorable journey, made even more significant following my meeting with historian Aman Nath. With his text and my photography, my first book, *Brahma's Pushkar,* was born!

My passion continued and I travelled to far-off places, shooting and interacting with my subjects. And when an old-time friend and accomplished travel writer, Rekha Sarin, approached me to shoot for Chai, it caught my fancy.

Once I saw her extensive research on the subject, I imagined myself amidst nature, in the lap of lush green tea estates, inhaling the aroma of tea leaves and capturing the excitement of the tea community and its produce. I readily accepted the assignment!

We decided to team up for a coffee table book on tea. Over the next few years we travelled extensively through the heartlands of tea, together and individually, experiencing the heritage and the Raj-era splendour of the world of tea.

I have tried the 'Perfect Shots' but truth is, there is no End to Perfection!

It has been a wonderful journey for me: the hesitant smile on the faces of the women tea pluckers, the sweat on the foreheads of the workers in the factory and the peaceful world of the tea estates, brought in another perspective to my life.

I do hope that somewhere amongst the pages of this book, I am able to take the reader into the beautiful world of this universally popular beverage Chai.

Rekha's
Musing

When I walked into a tea shop to buy Indian tea as a gift for my visiting German guests, I was overwhelmed by the cascade of eloquently described varieties of teas that were offered by the proprietor, a tea connoisseur. My imagination was immediately ignited and in my mind's eye, I could see the infinite beauty of the tea gardens, even as the aroma of the teas that I sampled pervaded my senses. During the course of my conversation, it struck me that tea is an art, a synergy between nature and mankind. And like all art forms, it is rooted in history. As a corollary, it has a strong aspect of culture, and in a sprawling country like India with distinctive regional options for tea, even more so. Given my inclination and years of writing in the genre of nature, travel and culture, it was perhaps, natural for the idea of this book to be born.

Having made an initial draft to include the fascinating aspects of tea that I felt I should research and share with my readers, I realised that this was a subject that could not be truly justified unless it was substantiated by visuals. Around this time, my good friend Rajan Kapoor had the launch of his book, *Brahma's Pushkar,* with stunning photographs by him and text by historian Aman Nath. I approached Rajan with my proposal. I detected the spark of interest in his eyes and soon enough, we teamed up.

As we progressed, both Rajan and I were drawn increasingly into this subject. We have shared the same enthusiasm—marvelled at the spread of the tea estates, the glistening fresh green shoots being plucked by smiling workers in the morning sun, the lengthening shadows cast by an orange sunset, dark nights with stars hanging bright revealing the silhouetted tea slopes, visits to the busy tea factories and tea tasting sessions—et. al. While I was jotting down my observations and conducting numerous interviews with the tea professionals, Rajan was creating compositions for his frames. Armed with heavy cameras, he had no hesitation about climbing up a machan or sneaking onto the roof of a village dwelling to get a bird's eye shot of the gardens. While he has infused the subject with life through his lens, I have sought to translate its many dimensions into graphic images with the power of words.

Much of my text is also flavoured with snatches of history for which I spent several hours in the stimulating silence of various libraries, absorbed in tracing the days of struggles and success of tea in India. I rewrote my initial draft a second time to assume more depth. However, at the end of it all, having taken stock of hundreds of photographs clicked for our treasury, including visuals acquired during overseas travels for the global aspects of teas, I wrote a third and final draft, this time, to amalgamate our final selection of photographs into the text.

This has been a labour of love. An impassioned endeavour to draw the reader into the true magic of tea that reflects the marvel of nature, human perseverance and intelligence.

Acknowledgements

The Indian tea industry is among the world's biggest, and is bolstered by hundreds of producers, large and small. The companies and names mentioned herein are merely a sliver, meant primarily to portray the essence of the subject. There are several other key players in the market and it is virtually impossible to do full justice to all. While recognising their contribution, we need to salute the lifeblood of the Industry: those thousands of workers who toil in the tea gardens to pluck the leaf, shoot-by-shoot, braving the vagaries of weather conditions, to earn their livelihood in the tedium of task.

I wish to clarify that tea statistics quoted in this book may vary over time; they are meant to give an overall image of the scale of the Industry.

At the end of it all I would like to submit, that despite my extensive reading and garnering of information, it would not have been possible to present this subject, but for the valuable inputs of all those expert tea professionals—heads of tea companies, tea planters, tea tasters, tea scientists, connoisseurs and enthusiastic tea lovers—who readily gave their patient guidance and answered my deluge of questions so graciously.

Several of the tea companies extended impeccable hospitality when Rajan Kapoor and I visited their tea gardens for photo coverage. The estate manager's wives maintained true tradition in being warm hostesses.

We also deeply appreciate the support extended to us by the Tea Board of India, especially in permitting us to present their logos that are featured in this book.

We extend deep gratitude to all those with whom we interacted in order to realise our work.

Aap ki Pasand Tea Company	Mr Sanjay Kapur, Managing Director
Mr Acharya, Peshwa	CEO Aasaan Pay. Founder, 'Think as a Consumer' Strategic Marketing Company
Apeejay Surrendra Groupg	Mr Karan Paul, Chairman, Mr Ashok Kumar Bhargava, Managing Director
Aquarius Marketing Pvt. Limited	Mr Dikshit Arya, Director
Chamong Tee Exports (P) Limited	Mr Ashok Kumar Lohia, Chairman.
Darang Tea Estate	Mr Naveen and Mrs Neeru Bhandari
Dharamshala Tea Company, Mann Tea Estate & Tea Gardens	Mr G.M.S. Mann
Duncan Goenka Group	Mr G.P. Goenka, Chairman
Dr N.K. Jain	Founder, International Society of Tea Science (former Director, Tocklai Research Institute)
Goodricke Group Limited	Mr Arun K. Singh, Managing Director and CEO
Goomtee Tea Estate.	Mr Ashok Kumar & Mrs Vinita Kumar
Harrisons Malayalam Limited	Corporate Office, Kochi
Hindustan Unilever Limited	Corporate Communication
Indus Beverage & Multifoods (P) Limited	Mr Savi Lamba, Managing Director (Past member, Technical Committee, US Tea Association)
ITC WelcomGroup Hotels, Palaces and Resorts	
Jay Shree Tea & Industries Limited	Mr D.P. Maheshwari, Managing Director
J. Thomas & Co. Private Limited	Mr Ashok Batra, past Chairman & Managing Director (now Consultant, Sustainable Value Chains, India) Mr Krishan Katyal, Chairman & Managing Director, Mr Viveck. S. Crishna, Managing Director, Mr Gautom Chatterjee, Executive Director

Makaibari Tea Estates	Mr Swaraj Kumar Banerjee
Mancotta Tea Estate	Mr Manoj Jalan
McLeod Russel India Limited	Mr Brij Mohan Khaitan, Chairman, Mr Deepak Khaitan, Vice Chairman, Mr Aditya Khaitan, CEO and MD
Mittal Teas	Mr Vikram Mittal—Tea Connoisseur
Ootacamund Club	Managing Committee
Planters' Club Darjeeling	Managing Committee
Rossell Tea Limited	Mr Chirinjiv S. Bedi, Managing Director
R Twining & Co. Limited	Mr Stephen Twining, Mr Jeremy Sturges, Senior Tea Buyer/Blender.
Tata Global Beverages Limited	Corporate Communication
The Assam Company Limited	Dr K.K. Jajodia Group, Chairman, Mr Aditya K. Jajodia, Managing Director,
	Mr K.R. Bhagat, Vice President,
The Imperial, New Delhi	Mr Vijay Wanchoo,
	Senior Executive Vice President and General Manager
The Kelagur Mathais Coffee and Tea Plantation	Mr Peter Mathais, Managing Partner
The Nonsuch Tea Estates Limited	Mr Bunny Mehta, Estate Manager
The Tea Board of India	Mr M.G.V.K. Bhanu, Chairman,
	Ms Roshni Sen, past Deputy Chairman
The United Nilgiris Tea Estates Limited	Head Office, Coimbatore
Tocklai Experimental Station	Mr S. Debnath, Microbiologist
United Planters' Association of South India (UPASI) Tea Research Foundation	Dr B. Radhakrishnan, Joint Director
Warren Tea Limited	Mr Vinay K. Goenka, Executive Chairman
Wellington Gymkhana Club	Managing Committee

I am deeply indebted to Dr Karuna and Dr Sunil Kumar, Professors of English, who helped me knit the text with their keen editing and constructive criticism.

Gratitude to Ann and Makoto Honjo in Tokyo, who shared my enthusiasm and drove me to the tea region of Shizuoka, besides arranging my participation in the tea ceremony that has been featured in this book.

Personally, my most comforting 'aroma' of support came from Deepali & Oscar, Dhiren & Bhamini who fill my cup of life with joy. Also Sarla Sarin, my 'other' mom, so gentle and understanding. Most importantly thank you, Deepak, my husband, for indulging my love affair with tea.

Finally, Rajan Kapoor and I sincerely appreciate the efforts of Ms Zahava Hirji, our Coordinator who threw herself wholeheartedly into our endeavour. With unflagging energy, she made arrangements for our travels to Assam and South India, setting up meetings and visits to the tea gardens. Her organized handling of all our book-related activities has indeed, been most helpful to the realisation of 'Chai'.

Photo Credits

Photographs	Source/Location/Courtesy
Tray with savouries & Tea kettle	Chor Bizzare, London
A lively discussion takes place over tea	Dolly's Tea Shop
Tea Party photographs	Home of Dido Chaddha, New Delhi
Tea Ceremony	Tea House & home of Uragami-san, Tokyo and Sawa Okano-san, Kodasan Temple, Yokohama
Painting of artists enjoying a tea party in Paris & Dutch tea tavern	Wikimedia
A tea shop in Hamburg	Tea Gschwendner Jungfernstieg 7, Hamburg
A tea garden in England	Wikipedia
Fast sailing clipper ships	Wikipedia
Twinings Van & Museum Entrance	Mr Stephen Twining, Twinings Tea Shop and Museum, London
Boston Tea Party	Wikipedia
Photographs of selective kettles	Aap ki pasand, New Delhi & Dido Chaddha
Array of Tea ware	Dido Chaddha
Image of Lu Yu	Wikipedia
Sectional display of tea varieties	Harrods
Tea Poster	
Gravestone of Charles Alexander Bruce	www.koi-hai.com
Nathanial Wallich, Lord Auckland & Robert Fortune	Wikipedia
Assam Company First Share Certificate	The Assam Company Limited
Maniram Dewan	Wikipedia
Engraving showing aspects of making tea in Assam	Wikipedia
Print showing Chowringhee, Kolkata	Wikipedia
Madras Regimental Centre Photographs	Madras Regimental Centre, Coonoor
Logo of Assam CTC & Assam Orthodox Tea	The Tea Board of India
Logo of Darjeeling Tea	The Tea Board of India
Logo of Nilgiri CTC & Nilgiri Orthodox Tea	The Tea Board of India
Logo of Dooars and Terai Tea	The Tea Board of India
Logo of Kangra Tea	The Tea Board of India
All photographs	Munnar Tea Museum (KDHP)
All photographs	Munnar Tea Museum (KDHP)
Tea displays & Twinings Tea Bar	Twinings Tea Shop and Museum, London
All photographs	Wikipedia
White Tea, Oolong Tea, Pu-erh cake	Aap ki Pasand, New Delhi
Selection of Teas at Harrods	Harrods
Packaged Blended brands from various countries	Harrods
San-cha Masala Chai	Aap ki Pasand, New Delhi
All photographs	Aap ki Pasand, New Delhi
Both Photographs	Aap Ki Pasand, New Delhi
End of a spa session at The Imperial	The Imperial, New Delhi
A yoga master strikes a posture for meditation	The Imperial, New Delhi
Aap ki Pasand Tea Parlour New Delhi	Aap ki Pasand, New Delhi
The Atrium at the Imperial	The Imperial, New Delhi
Recipes	The Imperial, New Delhi

Select Bibliography

Androbus, H. A. *A History of the Assam Company, 1839–1953*. Edinburgh: Privately Printed by T. and A. Constable, 1957.

Ananthanarayan, Ravi. 'What caused firms to wash hands of tea plantations'. *The Economic Times*, New Delhi, Dec 14, 2005.

Banerjee, Rajah. *The Rajah of Darjeeling Organic Tea*. New Delhi: Cambridge University Press, 2008.

Datta, Aparna. 'Teas from South India: The Nilgiris and Beyond'. *Crucible Chronicle* (2005), http://crucible-online.net/teatime/TeaTrekSouthIndiaTheNilgirisandBeyond.htm.

Griffith's Report on 'Tea of Upper Assam 1836' Report of the Commission on Tea Cultivation, Assam Tea Association. n.p.

Gazetteer of the Kangra District, 1883–84. Lahore.15 Aug 2001: Vol.1 Sang-E-Publications.

Gulab, Kushalrani. 'Do yourself a flavour'. New Delhi. *Brunch Hindustan Times Sunday Magazine*, April 15, 2007.

Gupta, Sujoy. *Four Mangoe Lane The First Address in Tea*. New Delhi: Tata McGraw-Hill, 2001.

International Journal of 'Tea Science' Vol. 3 (3& 4) 2004. Fiftieth Annual Report 2003–04

Ishizawa, Masao, and Ichimatsu Tanaka. *The Heritage of Japanese Art*. Tokyo: Kodansha International, Oct 1992.

Jhawar, R.S. *Tea: The Universal Health Drink*. New Delhi: UBSPD: March 2000.

Jones, Stephanie. *Merchants of the Raj: British Managing Agency Houses in Calcutta, Yesterday and Today*. Foreword by Lord Inchcape n.p : Palgrave Macmillan, May 1992.

J Thomas & Company Private Limited. *Tea Statistics*. Kolkata, West Bengal. 2009

Karmakur, Rahul. *"The Singhpo: The Cup that Jeers'. Teatime for the Indian soul'*. New Delhi, *Sunday Hindustan Times*, April 13, 2008.

Karotemprel, S; Dutta Roy, B. (Edited by) *Tea Garden Labourers of North East India. A Multidimensional study of the labourers of North east India* Shillong: Vendrame Institute. 1993.

Manton, Michael. *Camellia: The Lawrie Inheritance*. Edited by, under the Chairmanship of Keith Fitzgerald. U.K.: Camellia Plc. Wrotham. 2000.

Miedema Virgil and Metz Marilyn. *Heaven's Bright Land*. New Delhi: Rupa Classic India 2006.

Moxham, Roy. *Tea Addiction, Exploitation and Empire*. London (Hardback). Constable Sept.2003. Robinson (Paperback) Sept. 2004. New York (Hardback) Carroll and Graf, Fall 2003. Carroll and Graf, (Paperback) Fall 2004.

Notes on Tea in Darjeeling by a Planter. Printed by N.L. Roy: Scottish Mission Orphanage Press. 1888. India Office Library, British Council London

Okakura, Kakuzo. *The Book of Tea*. New York: Dover Publications. 1964

Papers regarding 'the Tea Industry in Bengal'. Findings of J.W. Edgar. Note prepared by A. Mackenzie, Officiating Secretary to the Government of Bengal, 29 October 1873 (Agricultural Department):Bengal Secretariat Press.1873.

Pettigrew, Jane. 'The Origins of Indian T*ea*'. Tea Muse Monthly Newsletter. Presented by adagio teas.August 2000 Issue. *http:// teamuse. com/article_000803.html*

Pratt, James Norwood. *The Dutch Invent* 'Orange Pekoe' Tea Muse Monthly Newsletter.Presented by adagio teas. May 2002. http:// teamuse. com/article_020501.html

Private Journals of W.M. Griffiths , F.L.S. Bishop's College Press, Calcutta. Privately published: London.n.p.

Priyadarshni ; Chacko, Thomas.Presentation, Research & Text. *Forest Gold: The Story of South Indian Tea*.Conoor. UPASI, (United Planters' Association of India) 2005.

Digby William, *Prosperous British India & Revelation from Official Records* by C.I.E. London T. Fisher. Unwin 1901

Pugh, Peter: *Williamson Magor Stuck to Tea*. Great Britain: Cambridge Business Publishing. 1991.

Report of the Commission appointed to enquire into 'the State and Prosperity of Tea Cultivation in Assam', Cachar and Sylhet 1868. National Archives of India Library

Reports on' the Tea & Tobacco Industry in India'. Presented to both Houses of Parliament by Commission of her Majesty,1874. National Archives of India Library.

Saberi, Helen. Tea: A Global History. London: Reaktion Books Ltd. 2010

Souvenir: '33rd Tocklai Conference on Tea Research & Development in The New Millenium12th–13th Feb 2001' Jorhat, Assam. Tea Research Association, Tocklai Experimental Station.

Taknet, D.K. *The heritage of Indian Tea: the past, present and the road ahead*. Jaipur: Executive Publications, IIME, 2002

'Tea Council, UK.Tea Facts.Woking, United Kingdom'. http:// tea. co.uk/teafacts

Tea in South India. UPASI. Tea Research Foundation. Tea Research Institute, Valparai, Coimbatore District.n.p.

The Book of Tea. Preface by Anthony Burgess. Paris. Editions Flammarion, 2005. Originally published in French as *Le livre du thé* : Flammarion, 1991.

Vohra, Dr.S.K. *My years in Tea. Life as a tea doctor was always colourful*. Kolkata. Contemporary Tea Time. Vol X1X.No. 2. June-Aug 2010

Weatherstone, John (1986). *The Pioneers: Early British Tea and Coffee Planters and Their Way of Life, 1825–1900*. London: Quiller Press 1986.

Libraries Consulted

National Archives of India Library, New Delhi
India International Centre Library, New Delhi
Japan Cultural Centre Library, New Delhi
India Office Library, The British Council, London

Websites visited

http://www.bigelowtea.com/universitea/history-of-tea.aspx
http://www.cancer.org/Treatment/TreatmentsandSideEffects/
ComplementaryandAlternativeMedicine/HerbsVitaminsandMinerals/green-tea
www.darjeelingteaboutique.com/happy-valley-tea-estate/
http://www.dutchdailynews.com/tea-good-for-your-heart/
http://www.glenburnteaestate.com
http://www.healthy-vitamin-choice.com/antioxidants.html
http://www.heritagetourismindia.com/
http://www.koi-hai.com
http://www.ootacamundclub.com
http://www.teaboard.gov.in
http://www.teafortealovers.co.uk/tea-history-garraway.php
http://www.waghbakritea.com/
www.woodbriargroup.com/
http://www.quotegarden.com/tea.html

Statistical Data

* Figures taken from The Tea Board of India
** Figures taken from J. Thomas & Company Pvt. Ltd.

Glossary

Aap ki Pasand: Translates in Hindi as 'Your Choice of Tea.'

Adha: Meaning 'half'. In the context of tea, half a cup measure, the other half being usually shared with a companion.

Atithi Satkar: Also connoted as *Atithi devo bhava* in India, derived from ancient times, meaning treating guests to the finest hospitality.

Avatar: A manifestation of a deity, an incarnation, used in this context to express complete transformation.

Ayurveda: An ancient Hindu science of healing based on herbal medicines and the principles of synchronising the body, mind and spirit with nature.

Bai Mudan: Silver Needle, a Chinese variety of white tea.

Banjhi phase: The resting period or the dormant phase of the shoot of the tea plant.

Bastis: Dwelling areas of lower income sections of society.

Bai hao: Chinese translation, 'white hairs', used in the context of the young tea bud being covered with fine downy hair.

Bihu festival: Ethnic festival of the State of Assam celebrated to herald the changing seasons and mark the corresponding phases of the agrarian calendar.

Brooke Bond Super Dust: A Hindustan Unilever tea brand. Super Dust implies the end product of the different grades of tea, the smallest particles release the strongest brew.

Bun maska: A colloquial term used in Mumbai to describe a sweet bun with a dollop of butter served typically in an Irani café along with tea.

Burra sahib: Great or big master. A form of address to mark respect, and was popularly used in colonial India.

Camellia assamica: Botanical name for a species of a hardy tree-like tea plant that is indigenous to the region of Assam in north-east India and yields stronger varieties of tea.

Camellia sinensis: Botanical name for a species of shrub or bush native to China whose leaves and buds are used to make tea.

Cha n garmo: Sweet hot tea made in Ladakh, with milk and sugar, similar to the style of tea in other parts of India.

Cha-bana: Style of flower arrangement used in the Japanese tea ceremony. The emphasis is more on the container in which flowers are positioned as naturally as possible.

Chai pani: In its literal translation, 'tea and water' it connotes tea and light refreshments. Figuratively may imply a tip.

Chang bungalow: In Assamese dialect, *chang* means *machan*, or a platform raised on stilts. These planters' bungalows were so named as they were elevated on stilts.

Cha-no-yu: Japanese tea ceremony, also described as the 'Way of Tea.'

Chasen: Bamboo whisk used for whisking powdered tea.

Chashaku: Wooden spoon used in a Japanese tea ceremony for scooping powdered tea from the container to the bowl.

Chashitsu: Japanese 'tea room'. Such spaces are designed specifically for holding the tea ceremony.

Chowkidar: A watchman who looks after the premises.

Chung houses: Rack withering of the leaf during tea manufacture, one of the methods employed for making the leaf flaccid and bringing about bio chemical changes in its composition.

Daisu: Portable shelf unit used for placing tea utensils in a Japanese tea ceremony.

Days of the Raj: Raj in Hindi means reign or rule. Days of the Raj infers to the period of British dominion in India.

Dhaba chai: Tea served in roadside tea stalls.

Dhaba culture: The experience of eating and taking refreshments in roadside restaurants or dhabas. A word used across India as well as Pakistan.

Dhansak: A popular signature dish of the Parsi Zoroastrian community. It is made of lentils, vegetables and mutton.

Dorje Ling: Translates as 'Land of the Thunderbolt', the name is believed to be given by Buddhist monks of an ancient monastery that was built by Lama Dorje-Rinzing in 1765.

Furogama: Brazier and tea kettle used for heating water in a Japanese tea ceremony.

Gaddis: Tribes of Himachal Pradesh, found mostly in Kangra Valley.

Gaiwan: Described as 'a lidded bowl'. This type of shallow bowl with a saucer is more suited for green tea or white tea.

Gamtcha: A traditional woven cotton cloth or towel for males, often used to wrap around the head, popularly used in eastern India and Bangladesh.

Ghats: Mountain ranges that run along the western and eastern coastline in the southern parts of the India.

Gong fu cha: Method of Chinese tea ceremony, its literal translation meaning, 'making tea with effort.'

Gopuram(s): Entrance gateway to a temple in South India. A hallmark of 10th–12th century architecture, the *gopuras* came to be monumental in size, with elaborate carvings.

Gorkhas (Gurkhas): A traditionally warrior race belonging to the Hindu Rajputs of Nepal. They derive their name from the warrior-saint, Guru Gorakhnath.

Gulab jamun: A popular cottage cheese-based dumpling that is fried and served in thick syrup. Favoured as a dessert in most countries of the Indian sub-continent.

Gurgur cha: Strong green tea with yak butter and salt made in Ladakh and Central Asia. It is churned in a long container to make a 'gurgur' sound, thereby earning its name.

Haats: A rural weekly market that sells an assortment of wares.

Hundi system: Indigenous banking system under colonial British India to facilitate money transfers, credit borrowings and bills of exchange for trade transactions.

Irani restaurants: Persian style cafes in India, with a typical atmosphere. Set up by Persian immigrants during the nineteenth century these are now dwindling due to the incursions of fast food.

Jalebis: A popular sweet in the Indian sub-continent. The flour batter is piped in concentric circles deep fried and dunked in syrup.

Janams: The tiny scale leaves of the bud that emerges from dormancy. These drop off once the shoot grows taller, and the bud with its dividing zone always remains on top.

Jats of tea: Type of tea bushes with reference to their place of origin, example, either China tea plants or the indigenous tea found in Assam.

Jhumar dance: A celebrative tribal group dance performed by tea garden workers of Assam.

Junshan Yinzen: White Peony, a China variety of white tea.

Kahwa: A special Kashmiri green tea preparation made with saffron, spices and almonds or walnuts. Varieties of preparation vary in different households.

Khansama: A male cook in India who generally acts as a house steward. A Muslim cook in a British household.

Kluntjes: Rock candy sugar used to sweeten tea that is typical to the region of East Friesland in Germany.

Kullad(s): Rounded terracotta/earthenware clay pots that may vary in size, used commonly to serve tea in wayside restaurants.

Lord Indra: God of rain and thunderstorms in Hindu mythology. He is also leader of the gods and the king of Heaven. He wields a thunderbolt and rides on a white elephant.

Mai baap: Translates literally as 'mother-father.' The term is used commonly to infer that the boss is the saviour, wholly in charge for all decisions.

Malis: In Hindi means the gardener.

Marwaris: Residents of Marwar, in Rajasthan. As several traders from this region migrated to Calcutta to set up business, they came to be referred to as Marwaris.

Masala chai: Literally translates as 'mixed spiced tea'. Made by brewing black tea with a mix of Indian spices.

Mem sahibs: Earlier used as a respectful form of address for European women who lived in colonial India. 'Mem' could be a derivative from 'm'am' and 'sahib' is Hindu or Urdu.

Meng Ding Huangya: Silver Needle yellow tea a specialty from China.

Murghi dak: A term meaning the 'first crow of the rooster', usually used in the tea gardens of Assam. It denotes the early start to the day, normally 6 am, garden time.

Neelakurinji: Botanical name, 'Strobilanthus kunthiana'. A shrub that grows abundantly in the Nilgiris and Western Ghats of India, and blooms once in twelve years to produce purplish blue flowers.

Noon chai: Translates as 'salt tea,' also known as '*sheer* chai', usually favoured by Kashmiri Pandits. It is pinkish in colour and is served with slivered almonds.

Pakoda(s): A fried snack similar to fritters, taken in South Asia. It is made by coating any vegetable or a hardboiled egg in a batter of gram flour and then deep frying it.

Panch: A word used in Hindi numerology for the figure five.

Parantha(s): Also referred to as *paratha* or *parautha*. An Indian flatbread made by rolling out whole wheat dough and pan frying it. Common in Punjab as well as Pakistan.

Pecial: Dialectic mispronunciation for the word, 'special.'

Pulum: Meaning, 'abundant water,' the word gives Palampur its name. As the town is circled by the Himalayan ranges, it receives plenty of rainfall.

Purdah: Derived from the Persian word for curtain or screen. The practice in certain Hindu and Muslim societies of screening women from men or strangers by way of all-enveloping clothes.

Raj: Literally meaning 'reign' in Hindi, this a term that is still used to describe the bygone era of British colonial rule in India.

Rajput(s): Hindu warrior ruling classes of north India. Their kingdoms were majorly in the regions of Rajasthan and Saurashtra, finally to be integrated into the Indian Federal Union.

Rang ghar: A colloquial term that translates as 'colouring room,' implying the change of colour of raw green tea to its coppery overtones in the fermentation room.

Rasgulla(s): A sweet made from balls of Indian cottage cheese and semolina, steamed and steeped in a sugary syrup. Especially popular in Bengal and Odisha and North India.

Rickshawala(s): Pullers of two-wheeled passenger carts, usually on a cycle, although sometimes a rickshaw may also be hand-pulled.

Ro: A hearth in a Japanese tea room, used for preparing tea during autumn and winter to keep it warm.

Salon de Thé: Tea rooms in the tradition of France that serve sandwiches, snacks and light refreshments with tea

Samosa(s): A popular snack in Asia, the Arabian Peninsula and the Mediterranean region. Made with a filling inside a fried or baked pastry, typically triangular in shape.

Samovar: A decorative metal urn used to heat water for tea. Its versions vary in Russia, Eastern Europe and Kashmir in India, but the mechanics of its design remain similar.

Seiza: Traditional sitting posture on a *tatami*, adopted by the tea master in a Japanese tea ceremony.

Sewa: A Hindi term for describing an act of compassion and service for the community or the lesser fortunate.

Sherpas: Ethnic Buddhist groups that moved from Tibet to Nepal. Originating from Himalayan heights, they are hardy and stocky, usually serving as mountain guides.

Sirdars: A Hindi or Urdu derivative from the Persian word, *sardar* denoting a high rank. In the tea gardens it would imply a superior or a supervisor in hierarchy.

Tamul (Paan): Areca nut eaten wrapped in betel leaves. In ancient Assam culture, offering *tamul* was considered as an act or a symbol of devotion, respect and friendship.

Tandoori roti: A whole wheat flat bread traditionally made in a cylindrical clay oven, with heat generated by a charcoal fire. It is popularly eaten with curries, lentils and grilled meats.

Tatami: Traditional woven rush mat used as a floor covering in Japan. *Tatamis* are made in standard sizes and room measurements are ascribed accordingly.

Teh tarik: Translates as 'tea hand pulled.' A preparation that originates from Malaysia by which the brew is poured in long motions from one cup to another to produce a froth.

Terroir: A French term signifying a set of physical and geographic conditions of a place to which an agricultural plant responds to produce a distinctive character.

Thakur: An Indian title meaning 'Lord', used generally to describe the head of a clan.

Thangka: A Tibetan religious painting on silk with embroidery that may depict the life of Buddha, a Buddhist deity or a *mandala*. Sometimes also used as a tool for meditation.

Tiffin rooms: Places usually found in South India where in-between snacks or a light lunch can be had. The word 'tiffin' originated in British India as a sort of Indian version of the afternoon tea.

Tokonoma: A recessed alcove, usually in a Japanese tea room, where objects of decoration like a calligraphy scroll or a flower arrangement are placed.

Topee(s): A pith helmet or hat, that was particularly in fashion during the British Raj in India as it was considered sturdy to ward off the tropical heat.

Tulsi: Known as the Holy Basil, revered in India from Vedic times. Known for its healing powers, it is often added to tea in Indian homes.

Udhagamandalam: Earliest reference to Ootacamund. In local Toda language, 'Ootaca' meaning 'single stone', and 'Mund' being the Tamil word for 'village'.

Vichaar: Advice or thoughts, usually in terms of guided wisdom.

Wazhawan: A formal, lavish banquet that holds a place of pride in Kashmiri Muslim culture, its culinary recipes may be secrets passed down over generations.

Wu Lung: Meaning Black Dragon, a variety of oolong tea from China botanical name Ocinum tenuiflorum. A variety of yellow tea from the Sichuan Province of China.

Zhisha clay: Purplish sand clay used for making Yixing teapots in China.

Index

A

accessories for tea drinking
    banbati, 28
      English crockery, 182, 232
       teapot, 20, 224, 235, 240, 242, 284, 296
       Yixing teapots, 225
Aerated Bread Company, 244
agency houses, 48, 51
Anamalai Hills, 180
Anamalai Hills estates, 55
Anderson Wright, 48
Andrew Yule, 48
antioxidants in tea, 54, 156, 264
Apeejay Surrendra Group, 52
Apeejay Tea, 170, 205
Apeejay Tea Limited, 52-53
Arbuthnot, Gillanders, 48
Assam, 48, 51, 53
    and Assamese culture, 48, 83, 293
    tea, 44
Assam Company (India) Limited (ACL), 51-52
Assam Frontier Tea Ltd, 52
Auckland, Lord, 36, 38
average per head consumption, 15
A.V. Thomas & Co., 110, 112

B

Balmer Lawrie Group, 52
banbati, 28
banjhi phase, 155
Banks, Sir Joseph, 35
Barua, Maniram Dutta, 35, 42
Barua, Rosheswar, 48
Bengal Tea Association, 38
Bentinck, Lord William, 36
Bhanu, M.G.V.K., 56
Birla, B.K., 108, 110
black tea, 134, 187
Blechynden, Richard, 235
blended & flavoured teas, 259
Bombay Burmah Trading Corporation Limited
        (BBTCL), 45
Boston Tea Party, 235
Briar Tea Bungalows, 116
broken leaf, 250, 252
Brooke Bond Lipton India Limited (BBLIL), 54
Bruce, Captain Charles Alexander, 72, 81
bubble tea, 245

C

Camellia Investments Limited, 52
Campbell, Dr, 42, 166
Carr, William, 38
Castleton Tea Estate, 95
catechins in tea, 194, 264-265
Chamberlain, Sir Neville, 184
Chamong Group's Tumsong Tea Estate, 98, 210
Chamong Tee Exports, 48
Champta Planting, 44
Chamraj Tea Estate, 66, 107
Chandrakii, Maharaja, 181
Chang bungalow, 59, 61
Charlton, Lieutenant Andrew, 36
Chennai, tea stall in, 28
Chikmagalur, tea from, 114
Chojiro, Raku, 242
chung houses, 192
Cinnamara Tea Estate, 72
Coonoor tea, 107
Coorg or Kodagu tea, 114
CTC tea, 131, 133, 249, 250, 252
cultivation of tea, 245
    Anamalais, 108
    Assam, 131
    Chikmagalur, 114
    Coonoor, 107
    Coorg or Kodagu, 114
    Darjeeling, 100
    extreme north east, 133
    Kangra Valley, 134
    Hassan, 125
    Himalayan ranges, 133
    Idukki District, 111
    Marwari community and, 48
    Munnar hills, 124
    Nilgiri hills, 44, 105
    North-West Frontier Province, 44
    Ooty, 107
    Palampur, 140
    Wayanad & Nelliyampathy, 108

D

Darjeeling Consolidated Tea Company Limited, 42, 52
Darjeeling Himalayan Railway Co. Ltd, 48
Darjeeling Planters Club, 182
Darjeeling tea, 85
Delhi

Ahmad Aziz's tea-shop, 25
Dashrath's tea-shop, 25
roadside chai, 25
d' Entrecolles, Francis Xavier, 231
Dewan, Maniram, 42
Dodabetta Tea Museum, 120
domestic consumption of tea, 15
Dooars & Terai tea, 131
Duncan Industries Limited, 53
Duncan Macneill Group, 51
Dunsdale Tea Estate, 107
dust, tea, 20
Dutch East India Company, 228

E
Empire & Singlo tea plantations, 52
English East India Company, 35, 214, 260
Europe, tea drinking culture of, 228
    England, 230, 232, 244
    France, 230, 235, 244
    Germany, 230, 232
    Holland, 230
exporting of tea, 245

F
fannings, 199
fermentation of leaves, 196
Finlay Muir & Company, 54
Ford, Napier, 45
Fortune, Robert, 42
Frys Fox & Company, 36

G
Garraway, Thomas, 232
Gaum, Bisa, 35, 42
genesis of tea drinking, 224
Gibbs, Richard, 36
Gillanders Arbuthnot, 48
Glendale Tea Estates Ltd, 116
global consumption of tea, 15
Goenka, G. P., 53
Goenka, Vinay, 53
Goenka, Vivek, 53
Gongfu Cha method, 240
Goodricke Group Limited, 52
Goodricke tea, 53
Gordon, G.J., 36
grades of tea, 198, 252
    Finest Tippy Golden Flowery Orange Pekoe, 250
    Flowery Orange Pekoe (FOP), 250
    Golden Flowery Orange Pekoe (GFOP), 250
    Orange Pekoe (OP), 250
    Pekoe (P), 250
    Souchong (S), 250
    Supreme Finest Tippy Golden Flowery
        Orange Pekoe, 250
    Tippy Golden Flowery Orange Pekoe
        (TGFOP), 250
Green & Black Kangra Valley teas, 134
green tea, 252
Greenwood Tea Estate, 62, 151
Griffiths, W., 36
gurgur cha, 20

H
Harrisons Malayalam Limited, 54
Hassan, 125
health aspects of tea, 263
herbal tea, 260
Hideyoshi, Toyotomi, 226
Highlands Tea Estate, 116
high tea culture of England, 244
High Wavys Tea Plantation, 45
Hindustan Unilever Limited (HUL), 54
Hooker, Dr Joseph, 42
House of Nusli Wadia, 54
Hung-wu, Emperor, 224

I
iced tea, 235
Idukki District, 111
'Imperial plucking' methods, 224
Inchcape Group, 51
Indian tea market, 56
indigenous tea plants, 36
instant tea, 260
J
J. Thomas & Company Private Limited, 202
Jajodia, Aditya, 51
Jajodia, Dr K.K., 51
James Finlay agency house, 54
Jameson, Dr, 44
James Warren, 48
janams, 155
Japanese tea ceremony (Cha-no-yu), 225
Jardine Henderson, 48
jasmine tea, 259
Jay Shree Tea & Industries Ltd, 52
Jenkins, Francis, 36
John Company, 233
Jorhat Tea Company, 38
Jungpana Tea Estate, 98

K

kahwa, 20

Kanan Devan Hills, 55

Kanan Devan Hills Plantation Company (P) Ltd. (KDHP), 45

Kelagur Coffee & Tea Estates, 114

Khaitan, Brij Mohan, 51

Khan, Genghis, 224

Khan, Kublai, 224

Kharjan Tea Estate, 52

kluntjes, 242

Kolkata

    Russel Dhaba, 28

Korakundah Organic Tea Estate, 107

Korakundah Tea Estate, 258

L

leaf segregation, withering, and rolling, 188, 192, 194

Lipton, Thomas, 233

Lloyd, Edward, 232

logos for Indian teas

    Assam tea, 148

    Darjeeling tea, 148

    Dooars & Terai tea, 148

    Kangra tea, 148

    Nilgiri Orthodox and CTC tea, 148

    of private tea companies, 149

Lohia, Ashok Kumar, 48

Louis XIV, King, 230

M

Mackenzie, A., 72

Macneill and Barry Ltd, 51

Macneill & Barry, 48

Magor, Williamson, 51

Maijan Tea Estate of Assam Company Limited, 170

Makaibari Tea Estate, 196, 258

Maneckshaw, Field Marshall Sam, 120

manufacturing systems, 188

Margaret's Hope Tea Estate, 54

Mariage Freres Company, 244

Marwari community, 48

Mathais, Peter, 114

Mathias, Diwan Bahadur S. L., 114

Mazarin, Cardinal, 230

McClelland, J., 36

McIntosh, A.R., 48

McLeod Russel Group, 51

McLeod Russel India Limited, 51

Mcleod Russel (India) Ltd, 51-52

McLeod Russel–Williamson Magor Group, 51

McLeod's, 48

mineral content of tea, 266

Ming Dynasty, 225

Mohammed, Hajji, 228

Moroccan Mint tea, 245

Mudis Group of Estates, 54

Munnar hills, tea from, 45

Munroe, J.D., 44

museum

    Dodabetta, 120

    Kanan Devan Hills Plantation Company's, 112

Mysore Coffee Company, 114

N

Nilgiri hills, 44

    tea gardens in, 108

Nilgiri Mountain Railway (NMR), 119

Nilgiris Tea Estate Company Limited (United Nilgiris Tea Estates), 54

Nilhat House, 216

Nonsuch Tea Estate, 108

noon chai, 20

North-West Frontier Province, tea ventures in, 44

O

Ochterlony, James, 108

Octavius Steel, 48

oolong teas, 140

Ooty, 44, 107

Ooty Club, 184

organic teas, 258

Orthodox tea, 107, 114, 249

P

packing of tea, 202

Parker, J., 38

Paul, Karan, 51

'Penny Universities', 232

Perrottet, M., 44

plantation workers' lives, 164

Planters' Club, 180

'Planters' Punch,' 180

Poabs Organic Estates, 110

Polo game, 182

polyphenols, 192

Premier Foods UK tea business, 54

Princep, William, 38

Pu-erh teas, 255

R

Ram, Senai, 48

Ramusio, Giovanni Battista, 230

recipes
    black tea poached egg with cha soba noodles and soya, 281
    blood orange ice tea, 274
    chai masala sorbet, 282
    citrus delight, 274
    coolers, 274
    Darjeeling tea and evaporated milk jelly with strawberry
        caviar, 282
    grandma's chai for cough and cold, 272
    green tea crème brulee, 283
    green tea marinated tofu in watermelon, ginger &
        pock choy, 281
    hot toddy, 276
    Kashmiri Kahwa, 272
    lemon ice tea, 274
    Masala chai, 272
    perfect cup of tea, 284
    rosehip tea consommé with star anise, topped with
        mint foam, 280
    spirited punch, 277
    voodoo, 277
Rikyu, Sen no, 226
rolling of leaves, 194
Ruia, A.K., 53

S
Sanjay Bansal's Happy Valley Tea
    Estate, 98
scented teas, 260
Sephinjuri Bheel Tea Company, 52
Sepon Tea Estate, 62
Sevenmalley Tea Estate, 112
Sevigne, Marquise de, 30
Sewpur Tea Estate, 48
Shaw, A.R. Gordon, 52
Shaw Wallace, 48
Shuko, Murata, 226
Silchar Club, 182
Singha, Raja Purinder, 42
Singphos, 42
sodium bi-carbonate, 20
sorting & grading of tea, 198
steeping tea leaves, concept of, 228
Stuyvesant, Peter, 235
Sullivan, Thomas, 235
Surianalle Tea Estate, 114

T
Tagore, Dwarakanath, 38
Tagore & Company, 38
T'ang Dynasty, 224

Tata, Jamsetji Nusserwanji, 54
Tata Global Beverages Limited (TGBL), 54
Tata Tea Limited, 55
tea auctions, 214
tea bags, 252
Tea Board of India, 56
tea ceremony/tea drinking habit, 243
    in British Isles, 244
    Chinese, 240
    Egyptian, 244
    European style of tea service, 244
    France, 242
    Germany, 242
    high mountain cultures (Tibet, Bhutan and Afghanistan), 245
    in Iraq and Jordan, 245
    Japanese *(Cha-no-yu)*, 226, 242
    Korean, 245
    Malaysian, 245
    in Middle East, 244
    Moroccan, 244
    Russian, 245
    Taiwanese, 245
    Turks, 244
tea estates/gardens
    Assam, 74
    Bessakopie, 42
    care for workforce, 173
    Darjeeling, 98
    Palampur, 140
    southern, 116
tea industry in India, 15
    accompaniments with
    Assam, 28
    Chennai, 28
    dhabas, 23
    ginger and bay leaf flavour, 28
    Gujarat, 31
    Hyderabad, 30
    Irani, 30
    Kashmir, 20
    Kerala, 30
    Ladakh, 20
    Mumbai, 30
    North Indian homes, 20
    popular variations, 20
    Punjab, 20
    Rajasthan, 31
    South India, 21
Tea Research Association (TRA), 72
tea stalls, 9, 25, 28
tea taster, 205

Teh Tarik, 245
The Thiashola Plantations Private Ltd, 108
Thomas Marten & Company, 214
Thompson, W.J., 36
tiffin rooms, 30
tisane, 260
Tocklai Experimental Station, 72
Tsung, Emperor Hui, 224
Tunstall, A.C., 72
Turner Brothers, 112
Turner Morrison, 48
Twining, Richard, 36
Twining, Thomas, 55
Twinings Pvt Ltd., 55

U
United Planters Association of Southern India (UPASI), 108
Uragami, Midori, 242
Uragami-*san,* 242

W
Wallich, Dr Nathanial, 34
Walter Duncan & Goodricke Limited, 52
Warren Tea Industries, 182
Warren Tea Limited, 54
Waterfall Ropeway Bungalow, 116
Waterfalls Estates Pvt. Ltd, 116
Wayanad & Nelliyampathy tea, 108
Wentworth Gold Mining Company, 108
Wentworth Tea Estate, 108
white tea, 254
Williamson, Pat, 51
Woodbriars Group, 114

Y
yak butter, 245
yellow teas, 255